Let's Build a Multiplayer Phaser Game

With TypeScript, Socket.IO, and Phaser

Oscar Lodriguez

Apress®

Let's Build a Multiplayer Phaser Game: With TypeScript, Socket.IO, and Phaser

Oscar Lodriguez
NIEUW-VENNEP, Noord-Holland, The Netherlands

ISBN-13 (pbk): 978-1-4842-4248-3   ISBN-13 (electronic): 978-1-4842-4249-0
https://doi.org/10.1007/978-1-4842-4249-0

Library of Congress Control Number: 2018965465

Managing Director, Apress Media LLC: Welmoed Spahr
Acquisitions Editor: Spandana Chatterjee
Development Editor: Laura Berendson
Coordinating Editor: Divya Modi

Cover designed by eStudioCalamar

Cover image designed by Freepik (www.freepik.com)

Distributed to the book trade worldwide by Springer Science+Business Media New York, 233 Spring Street, 6th Floor, New York, NY 10013. Phone 1-800-SPRINGER, fax (201) 348-4505, e-mail orders-ny@springer-sbm.com, or visit www.springeronline.com. Apress Media, LLC is a California LLC and the sole member (owner) is Springer Science + Business Media Finance Inc (SSBM Finance Inc). SSBM Finance Inc is a **Delaware** corporation.

For information on translations, please e-mail rights@apress.com, or visit http://www.apress.com/rights-permissions.

Apress titles may be purchased in bulk for academic, corporate, or promotional use. eBook versions and licenses are also available for most titles. For more information, reference our Print and eBook Bulk Sales web page at http://www.apress.com/bulk-sales.

Any source code or other supplementary material referenced by the author in this book is available to readers on GitHub via the book's product page, located at www.apress.com/9781484242483. For more detailed information, please visit http://www.apress.com/source-code.

Printed on acid-free paper

Dedicated to the hard-working and amazing developers who have contributed to JavaScript, TypeScript, Phaser, and Socket.io. Thank you for your time, dedication, and constant pursuit of perfection, which have created jobs and presented the gift of knowledge to the masses across the globe.

Table of Contents

About the Author

Oscar Lodriguez has been developing software as a freelancer for close to 13 years. During this time, he has worked with software giants such as Adyen, BNP Paribas, ebay, Bol.com, Schiphol, and Backbase. He has a bachelor's degree in computer science and is a motivated and avid learner who stays up to date with web industry standards. He has written three books and speaks regularly at Golang/JavaScript meet-ups in and around Holland.

About the Technical Reviewer

Sumit Jain is an MSc. CS postgraduate and a PhD in Computer Vision, Computer Graphics seeker. He is a founder of SummitGames Digital Entertainment Pvt. Ltd. He is an expert in technology domain and software applications and leads the entire software design and development process. He conducts workshops as a Speaker/Trainer in game architecture and programming.

"Game Development, is a process of writing a book, making a film and developing a software, all at once." –Sumit Jain

Acknowledgments

I would like to thank my partner, Debby Jong, for sticking it out with me and having faith that all would turn out great in the end, as writing this book was a challenging endeavor.

I would like to thank Rocco, my dog, for keeping me warm and providing company by sitting on my lap when I was hacking away at the keyboard late at night. Even though you are not going to read this, you are the best friend ever!

I would like to thank the great team at Apress for their pursuit of perfection. They have really helped me write the best book I could write, and I have gained so much knowledge based on their feedback.

CHAPTER 1

Introduction

First of all, I would like to thank you for purchasing this book. Writing this book has been a great experience for me, and I am excited to make this a valuable resource upon release. Planning, effort, as well as time have been injected into this project to make it as consumable as possible for developers with various skill levels. The goal is to provide technical know-how that instructs on what approaches may be taken when building a multiplayer game using Phaser, without losing too much quality in the process. The focus is currently on cleaning up the project and refactoring where need be.

Who This Book Is For

Some knowledge of programming is required, as I won't cover all of the language features that JavaScript offers. I will ultimately describe inputs and outputs of functions and why we need to do things a certain way. How the language and specifications work is something that is better left to another book, perhaps on Apress. Covering the basics of programming is something that has been done countless times by other books, schools, and courses. So to keep things focused, I will do my best to explain things as we move forward.

Topics regarding computer science will be touched upon briefly, but moving forward, some fundamentals of computer science are recommended. This course does require some knowledge of Git—more

© Oscar Lodriguez 2019
O. Lodriguez, *Let's Build a Multiplayer Phaser Game*,
https://doi.org/10.1007/978-1-4842-4249-0_1

specifically, Github. The knowledge you will need is how to clone or checkout a project and switching to a specific branch. Let's create a kickass game and learn a lot in the process!

How to Approach This Book

The material used by the project is best followed as a story. Don't skip ahead, as the story builds upon previous code and knowledge to allow you to have a successful working game in the end.

Skipping any chapter in between would mean you will lose valuable pieces of code that will make the project functional. If a topic feels like it does not suit you and you are considering copying and pasting the code in place, I recommend you give that a second thought.

The best way to learn is to properly digest the material and give it a meaning of your own. To help solidify your new learned skill, please experiment with concepts from this book on another project where you are stuck on a specific topic.

The sample code is found on the accompanied Github repo along with issues and potential fixes that might arise. The game will have additional changes outside of this book, this because, TypeScript, Socket.io and Phaser are both active projects and will contain updates. To keep up with these updates, use the accompanied online repository `https://github.com/codeOwl/Multiplayer-Phaser-game`, ever improving and getting better. It is important to know that the chapters hosted on github will be one chapter behind yours. This means when you are on Chapter 3, the branch you will checkout is from Chapter 2. This is because, in this specific example, Chapter 2 is the last result of your actions and you can continue with adding new features. I highly recommend checking out the start branch on the online repository by first cloning `https://github.com/codeOwl/Multiplayer-Phaser-game` and then checking out the start branch and building the game from there.

The book is comprised of lots of code. The best way to learn how to code is to be exposed to it as much and as often as possible. Simply put, the more you see it, the better chance you have of grasping and solidifying memory associations to implementation details.

What the Heck Are We Building Together?

Before starting on any journey or racing off to finish any goal, we must find out why we are doing it, get motivated, and tackle the tasks that will reach that outcome we so much desire.

We are set to take over the galaxy, or at least cause a mini-war in it, with our friends. The game we are building is to incorporate a real-time multiplayer game where you can race for the pickups and shoot your friends! There are no game rules attached to this game.

At the end, you will know enough about the implemented logic to apply your own game rules, such as first to five wins or Facebook connectivity with real leaderboards. The possibilities here are endless.

The key giveaway is not to build these rules but to give you the knowledge so can build them yourself. The whole point of learning is using creativity! I strongly believe in this approach and will include a bonus chapter of such a business rule to our game to give you a concrete idea. Learn, build, and destroy! Let's get started! A online preview version of the game is found here `http://codeowl.tech/game`. Use this link to allow another one of your friend to join so you can play together.

CHAPTER 2

Setting Up Our Development Environment

In this chapter we shall focus on getting set up and make sure we cover all that is needed for developing our game smoothly. The following are instructions to get you up and running with Node and Git.

Setting up Our Development Environment

Even though the game seems very simple and easy to code, there are a lot of moving parts, and it's good to digest them bit by bit instead of everything at once. Let's start with the tail of the dragon, which is the project setup.

If you already have node and git installed on your computer, skip the installing Node and Git section.

Install a decent code editor that will assist you at developing your game along the way. I recommend anything from JetBrains or Visual Studio Code from Microsoft. The good part is that Visual Studio Code is completely free and works really well out of the box with the technologies we shall be wielding. Let's dive into some explanation about Node.js and Git.

© Oscar Lodriguez 2019
O. Lodriguez, *Let's Build a Multiplayer Phaser Game*,
https://doi.org/10.1007/978-1-4842-4249-0_2

Node.js

The authors describe Node as an asynchronous event-driven JavaScript runtime, perfect for network applications that need to scale.

Git

The popularity of git has skyrocketed in the recent years as the de facto distributed version control system, focusing on speed, ease of use, and efficiency.

Prerequisites for starting this book:

- Install Node.js and Git.

    - Mac, Linux, or Windows users:

    - Install the latest for your system at `https://nodejs.org/en/download/`. Or, if you are tech savvy, I suggest you download NVM, which is a Node version manager. This makes it easier for you to switch between Node versions if you have a different project that will not allow you to install another Node version on your system.

    - To browse on the online repo, you can use Git to manage your code versioning. This can be downloaded at Git's official website (`https://git-scm.com/downloads`).

Note   If you are blocked on the where to start section, it means that you either need to upgrade your Node version or install Git. Installing Node and Git are some manual steps you will need to perform to get up and running with this project.

The Main Ingredient

For ease, I have created a getting started folder branch that includes the much-needed package.json manifest with all of the dependencies inside. This also includes an index.html file. When served via our server, this will request the correct libraries and resources. You can access this branch if you have checked out the project on Github by running git checkout start in your terminal while in your project folder.

Editors

Code editors are also software created by other developers that help developers to create software. You will need an editor to develop this game as it allows you to be more efficient at refactoring and getting type hints on your code. Ultimately, without going into too much detail, they will make you more productive as a developer and less prone to errors because of their features.

Feel free to use any common editors of your choosing. I recommend any of these (Sublime Text, Visual Studio Code, WebStorm, Atom), as they have good support for TypeScript. I like being a polyglot when it comes to programming languages, so I am using IntelliJ as my main IDE. It allows me to jump from TypeScript to Android development. I love that. To download an IDE or a code editor, just search for its name on your search engine of choice.

You can clone or fork the starter of this repository on Github (https://github.com/codeOwl/Multiplayer-Phaser-game). Once you have cloned the repo and assuming you have Git installed on your computer, checkout the starter branch, as it eases you into the project and you won't have to worry about dependency management.

Running the Project

Once all dependencies are installed, it is time to open up your package.
json file and see some handy scripts that are included that make your
development cycle life a tad bit easier. To run the development setup,
observe the following scripts and follow the instructions.

Listing 1-1. package.json

```
...
scripts": {
"precommit": "npm run lint",
"lint": "tslint -c tslint.json -p .",
        "start:dev": "webpack -w --env=dev & tsc -w --noEmit
        src/server/server & nodemon src/server/server",
        "build:release": "webpack --env=prod --optimize-
        minimize",
        "prestart": "npm i",
        "start": "webpack --env=dev && node ./src/server/
        server.js"
}
...
```

Having this insight means we now know a bit more of the process
installed behind the scenes of this game project. Running the command
"npm start" inside the root of the project will boot up the project and serve
it at your localhost port 3000.

Because you ran "npm start" the project installed itself and is running
successfully at the specified port above (port 3000). The project should
have started with a blank screen and the following text "Hi, I am being
served correctly". We shall be covering the nitty gritty details of sockets and
explore how they can help us realize this game.

The following section will explain a bit more about the development environment.

Running the Project in Dev Mode

Running the development is straightforward. Using concurrent jobs, we can run multiple services at once without starting a new terminal or we can spawn child processes. All of that is magically abstracted away!

$ npm run start:dev. This will set up the dev environment and a watch script that would detect any changes made to the program and then would rerender the application with your changes.

Our Front-End Architecture

Note we are not taking our massive node_modules directory with its contents into account. Your folder structure should reflect the following directory tree.

Note   Directories only show directories, not files or subfiles inside of those directories. The node_modules folder is most likely included in your build, and that is ok since it is at the root directory. (This is the same as the public and src directories.)

This illustrates the bare minimum we shall need in order to run code on the screen.

Note   If you have other files because of your current IDE, that is also fine. That is your IDE's way of saving the folder directory as a project so it can reference the relationships between modules.

Go ahead and run the project using the dev scripts explained here and let's see if your environment is working correctly without any error. Let's create a new file called "main.ts" and place it inside of the root folder. Later this is the main file that will include your entire application as an entry point. If you have a Java background, you can see it as your static main. If you do not, it is just the entry file of your application—also known as the shell.

Listing 1-2. main.ts

```
document.body.textContent = 'Hi, I am being served correctly';
```

Given you have your scripts running correctly in the background, you will see this as a result on your screen.

[image of results on screen]

Our Folder Structure

Our front-end architecture will be fairly straightforward. Looking at the directory image, we get a hint as to how everything will look at the end of the project. This is a good thing. Having a structure with no files inside makes you think like an architect and might save you a lot of time with refactoring in the future, when you are trying to figure out what goes where.

Diving a bit deeper than the surface area, here we have the listing:

- public ➤ The bundled application served through our server

  - assets ➤ Images and our css

  - dist ➤ Our bundled JavaScript files

- src ➤ Our project files

  - client ➤ Client-side logic for our game, including commands that will update the game-world

  - server ➤ Code that will run the server and open up a web socket for us

- shared ➤Shared code for both our client and server

Conclusion

It might seem like a small step. On the contrary, this is a huge step in the right direction! It means our server is also serving the static folder and serving the static files correctly to the browser on request.

This wraps up the setting up part. Let's just keep the momentum going on through the next chapter. We shall be touching a lot of TypeScript and general OOP topics in the following chapters.

CHAPTER 3

Orchestrating Our Domain Model

In this chapter we will be creating class diagrams for the following actors in our game: our game, the player, the phaser engine, and the controls. Code for this chapter is found on GitHub. (Considering you have the project running you can then checkout chapter/2 branch.)

The reason we need a domain model is that we want our fun little game to build upon a healthy, scalable architecture that allows for quick development iterations with as little to no noise as possible.

In this section we are solely focusing on the modules, models, and components we shall be creating, as with any project, as time progresses.

We will then think of new features we might want to add to it. Usually, it's not us that come with new features; we are always refactoring our own work and working away technical debt if we do not have a design pattern or framework we are using. By sketching out our model, we will intimately grasp our product and form a deeper understanding of its features.

After we have done this, we are going to utilize design patterns and define our objects by setting up interfaces to work it. Personally, I think this is the only approach to creating a project. Make sure you know exactly what you are building by mapping out all the separate components first and see if they all fit together before you even start coding.

© Oscar Lodriguez 2019
O. Lodriguez, *Let's Build a Multiplayer Phaser Game*,
https://doi.org/10.1007/978-1-4842-4249-0_3

In the end, you will make mistakes, but because you do not have to refactor the lot, as a bonus it is a cheaper and faster mistake to make. In the end because you have a working mental model on paper, it allows us to iterate over the ideas both then and come implementation time. Our ideas will have been reviewed multiple times, by ourselves and our peers. Always remember, get it on paper.

The Building Blocks

The following sketch (Figure 3-1) is of a simplified version of a class diagram. It represents classes alongside their methods and properties. This gives us a better indication of our project as a whole. The goal is to gain insight and clarity on what we are trying to achieve and if our methods and properties appear correct. Here is an example of how our class diagrams will look. Having a bit of background knowledge on UML or UML-like diagrams will certainly give you more insight. Here is a link to a good legend for UMLs: https://bellekens.com/2012/02/21/uml-best-practice-5-rules-for-better-uml-diagrams/?.

Figure 3-1. Simplified class diagram

In this example, we can observe the following:

The Game class will contain at least two properties.

- Actors

- Projectile

The Game class will be able to perform certain operations.

- Manage assets

- A game update

What these methods do can be mapped out as well. Using the knowledge we have gained from our first example, we shall be creating our first diagram, which will have these relational dependencies with each other.

Our approach will be to create all of the models and map them out separately. After that lay them out like puzzle pieces and build existing relationships between these models.

You may view it as assembling a piece of IKEA furniture. The first image you see are the tools you will need (which we discussed in Chapter 1; all of the pieces that you will need to assemble and the relationship mapping is done as a pre-step of implementation).

After all, you can only assemble what you are making after you are sure you have all the parts.

Creating Our First Model

Since we started with the Game class, let's keep working with it.

Properties

- -actors: Array

- -actor: Player

- -projectile: Projectile

- -game: Phaser.Game

Methods

- -manageAssets(): void

- -properties(): void

- -gameUpdate(): void

One thing you will quickly notice is the Game class only has private member variables and methods. Along with being private, the methods are all void functions as well, which means they do not return any value. They just perform a static operation once invoked.

The Player Model

With no player, you can have no game, but with no game, you will have not players. Next, let's look at the next most important class: the Player.

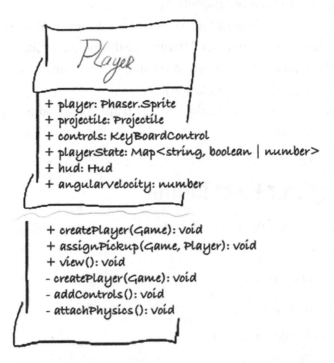

Figure 3-2. *Player class diagram*

Properties

- +player: Phaser.Sprite

- +projectile: Projectile

- +controls: KeyBoardControl

- +playerState: Map

- angularVelocity: number

- +hud: Hud

Methods

- +createPlayer(game): void

- +view(): void

- -addControls(): void

- -attachPhysics(game): void

The Keyboard Model

To control the player we are going to need some sort of peripheral. We are only building this game to be used with a keyboard, but you can easily extend or create more classes of your own that handle any other type of input. The keyboard is important, as it allows the player to move around the screen and interact with the gaming world.

Figure 3-3. *Keyboard class diagram*

Properties

- +gameControls: Controls

- -playerInstance: Player

Methods

- +update(): void

- Putting it all together

To create the simplest working model of our game, we need to take some more actions for integrating our game with existing libraries. We shall be using the powerful Phaser library to advance our game into the future with its extremely rich features. The reason I have chosen this framework was based on simplicity, popularity, and flexibility.

The most important part I find is that it includes a whole package of utilities that help you, as a game developer, to be productive really fast. Some of these features include a sprite engine, physics to control the game's collision, gravity or repulsion actions, animations, particles, and a handy camera that may or may not follow the player around the screen.

This will make it much easier for you as a developer to add an awesome feature to an already feature-rich application. Let's map out our game engine class, which will be Phaser.

Methods

- +preload(): void

- +create(): void

- +update(): void

The preload, create, and update functions are life cycle methods within the Phaser framework. Life cycle methods are functions that are called by the underlying framework (Phaser.js in this case), which runs at a specific point in time in the framework's life cycle. So for these methods we are calling the Phaser library to run on preload (before creating the game), on create (which creates the game world), and on update (updates the game world). Both the preload and create functions are called once, while the update function is called infinite times.

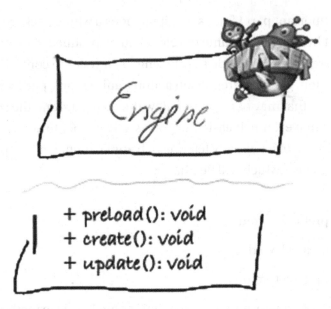

Figure 3-4. *Engine class diagram*

Our engine class will not have any properties because it will inherit the properties from our game. This will give us full access to the parent class and would be able to create the phaser engine inside of the engine class.

Like this, everything is nicely abstracted away. The Engine class diagram should then resemble the following image.

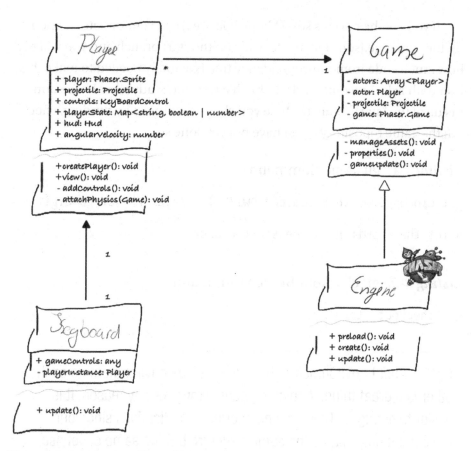

Figure 3-5. *Engine class diagram*

Creating Our Directories

Now that we have our basic models on paper for our game, let's start creating some directories in our project. Personally, I am a big proponent of starting everything from scratch if the opportunity to learn something arises. Around 5to 6 years ago, this was ok and reasonable to do.

These days it could cost you a day or even a whole week to get set up if you are thinking about setting up your own build-street and project from scratch. Solving NPM and dependency issues is something that is not easy and increases in complexity the longer the software is in production.

If you are the curious sort (I hope you are :)), in your directory, open up the "package.json" file inside while on the start branch and you will see how much code from the dependency tree is actually needed to make this a smooth ride. I recommend you hitch a ride and study what I have done inside of the "start" branch. Once you clone the project by running, check out the game repository if you have not yet done so.

Listing 3-1. git clone Command

```
git clone git@github.com:codeOwl/Multiplayer-Phaser-game.git
```

```
After that, switch to the start branch
```

Listing 3-2. git checkout Branch Command

```
git checkout start
```

Note   About environments: Having the same environment as each other is a great thing. If anything goes wrong for any reason, it is easier to debug and reduce engineering complications since our project not only shares the same structure but the same codebase.

Directory Construction

The next step we should take after digesting our mental models of our classes is to create a directory structure. There are two important things one must consider before mapping out a directory structure that makes sense not just to us but especially to others.

Some good practices for directory structures means semantically separating your implementation by groups. This means grouping related implementations or related functionality. A more complex structure might entail the need to group directories if assets in a directory are being shared by multiple implementors. A good approach would be to upgrade the feature in question's status in the hierarchy and promote it to the same level as the root implementors. We shall be using a similar strategy in our structure.

- public
    - assets
    - dist
- src
    - client
    - actors
    - player
    - controls
    - engine
    - game
- server
- shared (code shared between client and server)

Go ahead and validate if this is the structure inside of the start branch. We shall continue with the implementation of the code in the following section.

Conclusion

Having a clear blueprint of what we are building will make it considerably easier to start thinking in code. Having just made the UMLs, we have familiarized ourselves with the idea of how the game will function and where the dependencies may lay. In the upcoming chapter, we can finally focus on some code.

CHAPTER 4

Implementing Our Game Domain Models

In this chapter we shall be covering the following: introduction to Phaser.js and which features we will be utilizing. We will also implement the engine class along with the Game, Player and Keyboard classes.

We have not been coding yet, but this chapter will change all of that. We are going to implement the bare minimum to have a working game.

More features will be added to later chapters, as it is nice to see some results quickly. An introduction to Phaser is also pretty handy to give us a sense of what it is and why we need it.

About Phaser

Phaser is an awesome HTML5 game framework that works both on Desktop and HTML5-capable mobile devices. It's a framework because it offers all of the tools you might need to build a game, instead of a small subset of it.

Phaser ranges from a graphic to a gravity engine. It does so effectively by incorporating other open-source engines like PIXI (http://www.pixijs.com).

© Oscar Lodriguez 2019
O. Lodriguez, *Let's Build a Multiplayer Phaser Game*,
https://doi.org/10.1007/978-1-4842-4249-0_4

Being a framework, though, does have its drawbacks. The more features you include in one such engine also means the person wielding all that power needs to know all of its features and how to use them effectively.

Phaser supports all of the following features:

- **Sprites: A sprite engine that controls rendering based on images**

- Scenes and pre-loaders: Ability to tie your applications to multiple applications

- **Physics: Allow the game to be more realistic by adding weight to the world**

- **PIXI**: Rendering engine

- Animation: Gives an easy API to create amazing animations, fast

- Particle engine: Allow thousands of particles on-screen for a positive effect

- Sanitized camera controls: Makes it easier to allow the browser to focus on a specific action on the screen at any time (the player, the enemy, or any specific location)

- Mobile phone: Optimized for speed and allows gestures to be performed and ties them with actual functions of the game

- **Input** (keyboard, mouse): Standard and most used keybindings are already included for you out of the box

- Sound: Allows for an easy API to make the game perform sounds based off of actions

The features we shall be using to make our game are the ones in **bold**. Learning is done best through exploration and trial-and-error. I definitely suggest you play around with the other features once you have your space shooter up and running.

At the end of this book in a bonus chapter we shall allow mobile users to connect to our game and play as well. That means creating a smaller interface and being creative with user input.

Talking About Phaser...
Finally, Some Code!

In order to create any game using Phaser, we need to set up the phaser game world so we can make use of the powerful framework. The following code snippets will show and explain the steps for creating such an engine for our game.

Listing 4-1. src/client/engine/phaser-engine.class.ts

```
export class PhaserSpaceGame extends Game implements LifeCycle
{

        // The PhaserSpaceGame class will have one attribute,
        // which is the game itself created by Phaser to power
          our complete game with Phaser.
        private game: Phaser.Game;

}
```

Next we shall add our constructor.

Listing 4-2. src/client/engine/phaser-engine.class.ts

```
..
constructor() {
    // the game object in our class and passing in 4 arguments
    // width = 1024, height = 768,
    // Phaser.AUTO will auto detect what the browser is capable
        of (usually it's Phaser.CANVAS)
    // And lastly we pass in the same of our game, which is
        space-shooter
    this.game = new Phaser.Game(1024, 768, Phaser.AUTO,
    'space-shooter', {
        preload: this.preload,
        create: this.create,
        update: this.update
    });
}
..
```

This is definitely where all the magic happens. Once this gaming world is created by our chosen framework (Phaser.js), we can then leverage all the benefits the framework has to offer. Phaser needs to create our project (space-shooter), and once it has called all of the life cycles, it then has the correct dependencies in place for it to work correctly.

Notice how we are implementing the life cycle interface? Phaser offers us hooks to run code at specific time and places in our game life cycle.

We will take advantage of these life cycle hooks to populate the engine with our game. Read more about Phaser's life cycle here: http://www.html5gamedevs.com/topic/1372-phaser-function-order-reserved-names-and-special-uses/.

In the preload method we need to bootstrap the application.

Listing 4-3. src/client/engine/phaser-engine.class.ts

```
...
public preload(): void {
    // no need to set credentials for our requests are
        happening on localhost
    this.game.load.crossOrigin = 'anonymous';

    // set the game's background to space
    this.game.load.image('space', 'assets/background.jpg');

    // if any shot is fired with the image laser, register the
        bullet graphic
    this.game.load.image('laser', 'assets/bullet.png');

    // load the dust image
    this.game.load.spritesheet('dust', 'assets/dust.png', 64,
    64, 16);

    // load the explosion image
    this.game.load.spritesheet('kaboom', 'assets/explosions.png',
    64, 64, 16);

    // load the power-up graphic
    this.game.load.image('pickup', 'assets/pickup.png');

    // load the ship graphic
    this.game.load.spritesheet('shooter-sprite',
    'assets/ship.png', 32, 32);
}

public create(): void {
    super.properties(this.game);
    super.manageAssets(this.game);
}
```

```
public update(): void {
    super.gameUpdate(this.game);
}
...
```

TypeScript encourages the use of interfaces as well as helping us with types. Let's include the life cycle interface that Phaser offers us to our Engine class.

Listing 4-4. src/client/engine/lifecycle.ts

```
export interface LifeCycle {
    preload(): void;
    create(): void;
    update(): void;
}
```

The full code for our engine should look like that in Listing 4-5.

Listing 4-5. src/client/engine/phaser-engine.class.ts

```
import { Game } from "../game/game.class";
import { LifeCycle } from "./lifecycle";

export class PhaserSpaceGame extends Game implements LifeCycle {

    private game: Phaser.Game;

    constructor() {
        super();
        this.game = new Phaser.Game(1024, 768, Phaser.AUTO,
        'space-shooter', {
            preload: this.preload,
```

```
            create: this.create,
            update: this.update
        });
    }

    public preload(): void {
        const game = this.game.load;
        game.crossOrigin = 'anonymous';
        game.image('space', 'assets/background.jpg');
        game.image('laser', 'assets/bullet.png');
        game.spritesheet('dust', 'assets/dust.png', 64,
        64, 16);
        game.spritesheet('kaboom', 'assets/explosions.png', 64,
        64, 16);
        game.image('pickup', 'assets/pickup.png');
        game.spritesheet('shooter-sprite', 'assets/ship.png',
        32, 32);
    }

    public create(): void {
        super.properties(this.game);
        super.manageAssets(this.game);
    }

    public update(): void {
        super.gameUpdate(this.game);
    }

}
```

The Player Model

Create a new TypeScript file called "player.class.ts" inside of the player directory.

Listing 4-6. src/client/actors/player/player.class.ts

```
export class Player {
    // create your member variables like we glanced over inside
    // of our domain the player instance which will be a type of
    // Phaser Sprite
    public player: Phaser.Sprite;

    // The player can be controlled with a keyboard
    // KeyBoardControl class still does not exist at this point
        so your IDE should complain about it not being there
    public controls: KeyBoardControl;

    // playerState will keep side effects our player will get
    // during the course of the game. It will nicely embody all
    // of the states in one object

    public playerState: Map<string, boolean | number>;

    // Through Phaser this is used to control the ship's velocity
    // The math behind this is not going to be done by us, this
    // is why we decided to go for the usage of Phaser, which
    // will be more of a valuein your career.
    public angularVelocity: number = 300;
}
```

We are making some assumptions based on our domain models as to what the player class has and what it does.

Here we start with what we know, with utmost certainty, that the player contains and will be capable of doing. Next we shall add the methods that we have in our model. We won't fill out anything yet, but we will map them out and use our maps as guides for implementation.

Listing 4-7. src/client/actors/player/player.class.ts

```
export class Player {
    public player: Phaser.Sprite;
    public controls: KeyBoardControl;
    public playerState: Map<string, boolean | number>;
    public angularVelocity: number = 300;

    // Most classes need a constructor method but it is still
      optional
    // In our Player constructor we shall initialize some
    // members with initial values so we could use them
    // throughout our Player class
    constructor(private gameInstance: Phaser.Game,
                public playerInstance: any) {
        // Once we get information from the server we shall
        // create the player with the correct phaser game instance
        this.createPlayer(this.gameInstance);

        // We also save a local copy of the player created by
        // the server so we can reference the correct name and
          coordinate
        this.playerInstance = playerInstance;

        // Lastly we shall be needing a place to keep all of our
        // side effects. This will serve as a common container
        // for all of our player states (ex: number of bullets
        // fired, is the player moving?, etc)
        this.playerState = new Map();
    }
```

```
// We shall need a way to create our players which are
// requested through other classes in our game Having a
// factory or a centralized way to create a player means
// that we run little risk of duplicating code
public createPlayer(): void {

}

// Our game will have some sort of loot drop system.
// If a player picks up a loot, we shall assign it to the
// player who picked it up
public assignPickup(): void {

}

// As changes happen through the game world, the player
// view will have to reflect these changes. The view is
// nothing more than a graphical representation of our
   awesome spaceship
public view(): void {

}

// Once we instantiate the player we must attach some
   controls to it!
private addControls(): void {

}

// Let's add an extra method to attach physics to our player
// Physics will be provided by Phaser's arcade implementation
// and will add a lot of liveliness to our game.
private attachPhysics(): void {

}

}
```

Since creating the player is the most trivial, let's create the logic for this method first.

Listing 4-8. src/client/actors/player/player.class.ts

```
...
// When Instantiating a new player instance, we shall be needing
// the game world as an instance. This is so we can inject it
// directly into Phaser's created canvas.
public createPlayer(gameInstance): void {
    // Attach the controls to this player's game world
    this.addControls();

    // Add the player to our world through Phaser.
    this.player = gameInstance.add.sprite(
        100, 100, 'shooter-sprite'
    );

    // Set the anchor to center of the sprite
    this.player.anchor.setTo(0.5, 0.5);

    // To attach physics to our sprite, we need to call this
        private class
    this.attachPhysics(gameInstance);
}
...
```

Phaser Arcade Physics

Before we go into integrating more of Phaser's features, Let's take time to talk about Phaser's physics arcade engine. The arcade engine is one of the simplest implementations of physics inside of the phaser framework. It is all we shall need to implement our awesome space shooter.

It will save us tons of performance and our game will not require a more complicated/feature-rich physics implementation. To illustrate a simple difference between Arcade and the p2 engine, consider the image in Figure 4-1.

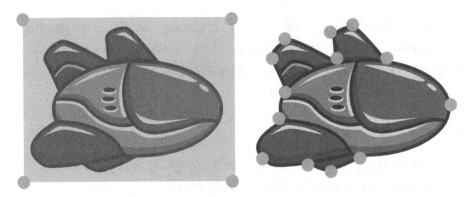

Figure 4-1. *src/client/game/game.class.ts*

The image on the left is showing the Arcade model, and the image on the right is showing the more complex p2 engine model. Both are great, p2 is just more detailed, and with Arcade it is more performant as it has less vector points for the collision body.

It is also much easier to implement and will allow us to see results much quicker. To make our spaceship aware in the game world, we shall need to attach Phaser's physics to it. Let's go ahead and add this to our spaceship class. In the next class we shall incorporate these calls to enable Phaser.js to add physics to any created ship.

Listing 4-9. src/client/actors/player/player.class.ts

```
...
// Pass the game instance so we can to the physics method to
// give it the correct phaser game instance to work with. Do
// not worry about this too much since we shall be covering
   this in the following models
```

```
private attachPhysics(gameInstance): void {
    // using the Phasers game instance method we are attaching
    // to the world and setting the physics mode to arcade
    gameInstance.physics.enable(this.player, Phaser.Physics.
    ARCADE);

    // Let the player respect the browser edges. If you fly
    //     further than the allocated space you will bounce and be
    //     forced back into the game world
    this.player.body.collideWorldBounds = true;

    // If anything collides against our player, this is the
    //     bounciness setting
    this.player.body.bounce.setTo(10, 10);

    // We are in space so let's set our space body to 0 gravity
    this.player.body.gravity.y = 0;

    // we do not want our spaceship to just stop out of nowhere
    // when we stop accelerating. This drag indicates the
    // momentum we bring along when flying around the screen
    this.player.body.drag.set(80);

    // Our max speed
    this.player.body.maxVelocity.set(100);

    // When another ship collides against us, we want to have a
    //     reaction to that
    // This means we should be moveable inside of the phaser
    //     framework.
    this.player.body.immovable = false;
}
...
```

That will conclude our player class. The end result should look like that in Listing 4-10.

Listing 4-10. src/client/actors/player/player.class.ts

```
export class Player {
    public player: Phaser.Sprite;
    public projectile: Projectile;
    public controls: KeyBoardControl;
    public playerState: Map<string, boolean | number>;
    public angularVelocity: number = 300;

    constructor(private gameInstance: any, public
    playerInstance: any) {
        this.createPlayer(this.gameInstance);
        this.playerState = new Map();
    }

    public createPlayer(gameInstance): void {
        this.addControls();
        this.player = gameInstance.add.sprite(
            100,
            100,
            'shooter-sprite'
        );
        this.player.id = "1";
        this.player.anchor.setTo(0.5, 0.5);
        this.player.animations.add('accelerating',
        [1, 0], 60, false);
        this.player.name = "your name";
        this.attachPhysics(gameInstance);
    }
```

```
public assignPickup(game, player?): void {
    this.projectile = new Projectile(game, player.
    player);
    this.playerState.set('ammo', this.projectile.
    bulletCount);
}

public view(): void {
    this.controls.update();
}

private addControls(): void {
    this.controls = new KeyBoardControl(this.
    gameInstance, this);
}

private attachPhysics(gameInstance): void {
    gameInstance.physics.enable(this.player, Phaser.
    Physics.ARCADE);
    this.player.body.collideWorldBounds = true;
    this.player.body.bounce.setTo(10, 10);
    this.player.body.gravity.y = 0;
    this.player.body.drag.set(80);
    this.player.body.maxVelocity.set(100);
    this.player.body.immovable = false;
}
}
```

The Game Model

Our little spaceship needs a world to live in. It's impossible to shoot your friends when you do not both live in the same galaxy.

Listing 4-11. src/client/game/game.class.ts

```
export class Game {

    // The game world members

    // The game world will serve as our main application
    // container. It will be the communication layer between
    // our server and our client. With that in mind it makes
       it a fairly busy class.

    // first we are going to need a place where we store all
    // of the players on the client-side
    private actors: Array;

    // Every game should also have a protagonist. Our main
       protagonist will be stored like so
    private actor: Player;

    // The protected member variable will make much more
       sense once we have created the Phaser Game engine.
    protected game: Phaser.Game;

}
```

Let's now add the methods created in our game. Remember that the Game will never be instantiated, because the Phaser engine class we have created first is extending and drawing properties for this class. So that means we can also set up this class to have nice, compact, protected methods that can only be implemented in subclasses.

Listing 4-12. src/client/game/game.class.ts

...

```
protected manageAssets(): void {
        // Use the manageAssets class control our game
            creational lifecycle
        // Which mainly means to turn on our event listeners!
 }

protected gameUpdate(): void {
        // Our busiest class! The update will be called 60 frames
        // per second to update our game mode and our
        // subscriptions mentioned above. Think of it as the
            game's heartbeat. Now that everything is in place
        The heart pumps life to all of our organs (modules) 12
}

protected properties(): void {
        Implementing our game domain models
        // We also should call the properties methods on the
        // create lifecycle of the engine. This makes it much
        // easier to set all of our game properties in one
            place. Since it is our "game" properties, we should
        // either put it in a game.config file or in the game
            class directly.
}
...
```

In the end, our full game class will be much more complicated than this. But let's take it one step at a time. It's better to introduce certain values first and then take our time to upgrade the already earned knowledge, instead of everything at once.

Listing 4-13. src/client/game/game.class.ts

```
export class Game {
        // since we do not have models yet. To stop your IDE from
            complaining
        // we shall change the types to any for now, until we
            have created our
        // game models.
        private actors: Array;
        private actor: any;
        protected game: Phaser.Game;

        protected manageAssets(): void { }

        protected gameUpdate(): void {
                // If the actor exists in our game. let's update it!
                // We shall be making the controls in the next
                    section when we
                // implement our keyboard class
                if (this.actor && this.actor.controls) {
                this.actor.view();
                }
        }

        protected properties(): void {
                // The properties below are mainly configurations
                // the Phaser framework offers to use.

                // Since we are making a multiplayer game it's
                // crucial we are always updating the world.
                // Removing the disability change means that our
                    game will always be running, even if we switch
                // from windows whilst using our browsers
                this.game.stage.disableVisibilityChange = true;
```

```
// We have preloaded the space texture, here we are
   setting it in
// our game
this.game.add.tileSprite(
      0, 0,
      this.game.width,
      this.game.height,
      'space'
);
this.game.add.sprite(0, 0, 'space');

// We want our game to be fast and furious! 60FPS
   all the things
this.game.time.desiredFps = 60;

// clear before render will give us better
   performance because we
// have a static background
this.game.renderer.clearBeforeRender = false;

// Set the correct physics engine for our game and
this.game.physics.startSystem(Phaser.Physics.ARCADE);

   }

}
```

The Keyboard Model

Finally we shall need a way of controlling our player on the screen. Let's go for the easiest one to implement—the input module! Let's first add our instance properties of the keyboard, which will be used as our input module of choice.

Listing 4-14. src/client/controls/keyboard.class.ts

```
export class KeyBoardControl {
        // The purpose of the KeyBoardControl class is to
          delegate any player
        // input to here. This keeps our logic in one central
          place when it
        // comes to character movement and actions

        // since we do not have any models yet, create the
          gameControls method
        // and set it to any and an empty object
        public gameControls: Controls;
}
```

Inside of the same directory, we shall create a model for our controls to help us in the future of what the control object will require.

Listing 4-15. src/client/controls/keyboard.model.ts

```
export interface Controls {
        // Having an interface will help us in the future as it
          will hint to us
        // and other developers what our model is expecting in
          the end
        cursors: Phaser.CursorKeys;
        fireWeapon: Phaser.Key;
}
```

Now we can mainly focus on creating the functionality of the keyboard itself. Let's include the methods that will govern the control of our spaceship. Creating a good API requires a lot of sympathy for the developers, integrators, and your future self. So it is on us to come with meaningful and logical names for our methods.

Listing 4-16. src/client/controls/keyboard.model.ts

```
// add the player class to the imports
import {Player} from '../actors/player/player.class';

// since the keyboard will not be called inside of this file,
let's export it
export class KeyBoardControl {

    public gameControls: Controls;

    // The keyboard class has two dependencies.
    // The game world and the player instance
    constructor(private gameInstance: any, private
    playerInstance: Player) {
        // Add the following definition of our gameControls
        this.gameControls = {
            // Keep records of the phaser's input keys in our
                implementation
            cursors: this.gameInstance.input.keyboard.
            createCursorKeys(),

            // We do not yet have the fire feature, but it's
                good to add the
            // functionality hook for it already. We are
                telling Phaser at
            // this point to react to spacebar input presses.
            fireWeapon: this.gameInstance.input.keyboard.addKey(
                Phaser.KeyCode.SPACEBAR
            )
        }
    }
```

```
// The heartbeat of the keyboard class is being called
   outside.
// The game-loop created by phaser is responsible for
   calling the update
// method on every iteration. Which is what we of course
   hope, 60fps.
public update(): void {

    // Wrap any logic here for when the player is alive
    if (this.playerInstance.player.alive) {

        // Update the player state if the player has fired
           a shot
        this.playerInstance.playerState.set('fire', false);

        // Add a const for the player velocity
        // To avoid a long method path add a small variable
           to capture
        // our static element of the player's velocity speed
        const vel = this.playerInstance.angularVelocity;

        // If the player is moving do the following
        if (this.gameControls.cursors.up.isDown) {

            // Get the current rotation of the player and
               allow the
            // player to move forward within the bounded
               acceleration
            // constraints
            this.gameInstance.physics.arcade.
            accelerationFromRotation(
                this.playerInstance.player.rotation,
                100,
                this.playerInstance.player.body.acceleration);
```

```
        // Let's update the state if the player is
            moving so we can
        // notify the game world and later the other
            players that
        // this current player is currently moving.
        this.playerInstance.player.animations.
        play('accelerating');
        this.playerInstance.playerState.set('moving',
        true);

    } else {
        // Our ship can only accelerate forward in
            space at the
        // moment, so if the player is not moving at
            all, we can set
        // the acceleration to 0 and reset the moving
            state back to
        // false. This lets the other players and the
            game-world know
        // that this spaceship is not moving anymore.
        this.playerInstance.player.body.acceleration.
        set(0);
        this.playerInstance.playerState.set('moving',
        false);
    }

    // Logic for when the player is turning
    if (this.gameControls.cursors.left.isDown) {

        // Add the negative value to the Angular's
            velocity to
        // update the character when turning left.
```

```
        this.playerInstance.player.body.angularVelocity
        = -vel;

    } else if (this.gameControls.cursors.right.isDown) {

        // Add the value to the Angular's velocity to
        // update the character when turning right
        this.playerInstance.player.body.
        angularVelocity = vel
    } else {

        // If the user is not turning left, nor right
            that means
        // that the user is currently not turning at
            all. So let's
        // set the current degree to 0
        this.playerInstance.player.body.
        angularVelocity = 0;

    }
  }
 }
}
```

Conclusion

Awesome! Now that all of the parts are created separately on their separate islands, let's hook them together in the upcoming chapter. We are extremely close to actually seeing something on the screen. Before we get too eager to see our work, it is good to get intimately associated with the code. This will give you a better insight into our overall structure and how you can add your own features.

In the following chapter, we will concentrate on getting a visibly working program.

CHAPTER 5

Seeing It In Action

It's that exciting time where we can actually see what we have been created on screen! In this chapter, we shall be covering how to create relationship between our implementations by putting all we have done together to work in unison.

Code for this chapter is found on GitHub (`https://github.com/codeOwl/Multiplayer-Phaser-game/tree/chapter/4`). This will let you view what you already should have running locally. If you run "git checkout chapter/4" in your terminal, you will checkout this chapter of the project. While we have focused on the previous chapters to get the code into the right place, this chapter will mostly focus on existing code and how to make them interact with one another.

Hooking it All up Together

This is the easy part. TypeScript allows us to use ES15+ imports in our code. If you are unfamiliar with this concept of "imports," you can read more about it here (`https://developer.mozilla.org/en-US/docs/Web/JavaScript/Reference/Statements/import`). I recommend clicking and reading a bit more on that even if you are a seasoned developer who has been working with JS for a couple of years. There are probably some features you did not know about before.

© Oscar Lodriguez 2019
O. Lodriguez, *Let's Build a Multiplayer Phaser Game*,
https://doi.org/10.1007/978-1-4842-4249-0_5

We should go ahead and review the classes we have created so far and add some adjustments so they know to create associations with each other during the compilation phase. Do not worry about which adjustments just yet, as they will be covered in the code section with their corresponding descriptions. This is a lot of jargon for: "Let's add some imports." Let's look at our game final game engine file.

Listing 5-1. src/client/engine/phaser-engine.class.ts

```
import { Game } from "../game/game.class";
import { LifeCycle } from "./lifecycle";

export class PhaserSpaceGame extends Game implements LifeCycle
{

    private game: Phaser.Game;

    constructor() {
        super();
        this.game = new Phaser.Game(1024, 768, Phaser.AUTO,
        'space-shooter', {
            preload: this.preload,
            create: this.create,
            update: this.update
        });
    }

    public preload(): void {
        const game = this.game.load;
        game.crossOrigin = 'anonymous';
        game.image('space', 'assets/background.jpg');
        game.image('laser', 'assets/bullet.png');
        game.spritesheet('dust', 'assets/dust.png', 64, 64, 16);
```

```
    game.spritesheet('kaboom', 'assets/explosions.png', 64,
    64, 16);
    game.image('pickup', 'assets/pickup.png');
    game.spritesheet('shooter-sprite', 'assets/ship.png',
    32, 32);
  }

  public create(): void {
    super.properties(this.game);
    super.manageAssets(this.game);
  }

  public update(): void {
    super.gameUpdate(this.game);
  }

}
```

The only addition is that we have added the import to our game class.
This way we tell the phaser engine class to use our game class specifically.

Our game class also has an association with our player class, as it is the
area where our game world and the player interact with one another. Our
game class should reflect what is shown in Listing 5-2.

Listing 5-2. src/client/actors/player/player.class.ts

```
import {Player} from '../actors/player/player.class';

declare const window: any;

export class Game {
    private actors: Array;
    private actor: Player;
```

```
protected manageAssets(game): void {
    this.actors = [];
    // later will contain all of our game logic code
    this.actor = new Player(game);
}

protected gameUpdate(game): void {
    if (this.actor && this.actor.controls) {
        this.actor.view();
    }
}

protected properties(game): void {
    game.stage.disableVisibilityChange = true;
    game.add.tileSprite(0, 0, game.width, game.height,
    'space');
    game.add.sprite(0, 0, 'space');
    game.time.desiredFps = 60;
    game.renderer.clearBeforeRender = false;
    game.physics.startSystem(Phaser.Physics.ARCADE);
}
}
```

Our game has an engine! That means we can go on and start hooking up our player to the game world.

Listing 5-3. src/client/actors/player/player.class.ts

```
import {KeyBoardControl} from '../../controls/keyboard.class';

export class Player {
    public player: Phaser.Sprite;
    public controls: KeyBoardControl;
```

```
public playerState: Map;
public angularVelocity: number = 300;

constructor(private gameInstance: Phaser.Game,
            public playerInstance: any) {

    // the any type for the player instance will be
       resolved soon
    this.createPlayer(this.gameInstance);
    this.playerState = new Map();
}

public createPlayer(gameInstance): void {
    this.addControls();
    this.player = gameInstance.add.sprite(
        100, 100, 'shooter-sprite'
    );
    this.player.id = '1';
    this.player.anchor.setTo(0.5, 0.5);
    this.player.animations.add('accelerating', [1, 0],
    60, false);
    this.player.name = "Your name";
    this.attachPhysics(gameInstance);
}

public view(): void {
    this.controls.update();
}

private addControls(): void {
    this.controls = new KeyBoardControl(this.
    gameInstance, this);
}
```

```
    private attachPhysics(gameInstance): void {
        gameInstance.physics.enable(this.player, Phaser.
        Physics.ARCADE);
        this.player.body.collideWorldBounds = true;
        this.player.body.bounce.setTo(10, 10);
        this.player.body.gravity.y = 0;
        this.player.body.drag.set(80);
        this.player.body.maxVelocity.set(100);
        this.player.body.immovable = false;
    }
}
```

There is one more step to perform after setting up our keyboard class. This is to include the "main.ts" file that will serve as our application entry file. Before we get to the concepts of entry files, let's make sure our keyboard class has all the dependencies it needs to work.

Listing 5-4. src/client/controls/keyboard.class.ts

```
import {Player} from '../actors/player/player.class';
import {Controls} from './keyboard.model';

export class KeyBoardControl {
    public gameControls: Controls;

    constructor(private gameInstance: Phaser.game,
                private playerInstance: Player) {
        const space = Phaser.KeyCode.SPACEBAR;
        this.gameControls = {
            cursors: this.gameInstance.input.keyboard.
            createCursorKeys(),
            fireWeapon: this.gameInstance.input.keyboard.
            addKey(space)
        }
    }
```

```
public update(): void {
    if (this.playerInstance.player.alive) {
        this.playerInstance.playerState.set('fire', false);
        const vel = this.playerInstance.angularVelocity;
        if (this.gameControls.cursors.up.isDown) {
            this.gameInstance.physics.arcade.
            accelerationFromRotation(
                this.playerInstance.player.rotation,
                100,
                this.playerInstance.player.body.acceleration);
            this.playerInstance.player.animations.
            play('accelerating');
            this.playerInstance.playerState.set('moving', true);
        } else {
            this.playerInstance.player.body.acceleration.set(0);
            this.playerInstance.playerState.set('moving',
            false);
        }

        if (this.gameControls.cursors.left.isDown) {
            this.playerInstance.player.body.angularVelocity
            = -vel;
        } else if (this.gameControls.cursors.right.isDown)
{

            this.playerInstance.player.body.angularVelocity
            = vel;
        } else {
            this.playerInstance.player.body.angularVelocity = 0;
        }

    }
}
}
```

Finally, we discussed a bit about our project entry file. This is the main application shell whose sole job is to load the application and instantiate it. The main will import our index, which will import our whole game. Applications are not that far away from novels. Consider the following analogy. A book contains the game. The book is the main object, so let's call it the main. Inside of the main object, you will have an index that is aware of all the parts of the book. This will be our "index.ts" file. Let's start with the index file.

Listing 5-5. src/client/index.ts

```
import {PhaserSpaceGame} from './client/engine/phaser-engine.class';
new PhaserSpaceGame();
```

Voila! We are all done. We can now see our initial game in action by running the following in our terminals. Head over to the project directory with your terminal and run the following command.

```
Inside of our terminal or prompt, let's run the following command:
"npm start"
```

Conclusion

You may now view your game with the following on your localhost port 3000. You can also change the standard port inside of our "server.ts" file. This way you can manage which port is best suitable for you. It's pretty cool that we have our game running, but it hardly feels or seems like a game at all at this point in time. We should add more game functionality in the following chapter so we can then show off to our friends!

CHAPTER 6

Projectiles!

We made it to Chapter 6! This is where we shall add the fun parts to the game. We shall be setting up the props and also assigning new features to our existing sprites! We shall also look at how we are allowing the user to fire her laser beams.

Code for this chapter is found on GitHub or by checking out the chapter/5 branch. Our spaceship is created and can move around the screen. Let's add a new feature that allows our spaceship to shoot! Phaser comes with a handy ability to shoot/fire feature, as it has a built-in method that we can call to assist us when adding our weapon.

Let's set up a Projectile class that implements the idea of something being launched from our spaceships. We shall only be implementing the laser projectile. You are here encouraged to build homing seeking rockets that follow the nearest enemy's x,y coordinates! To start creating a projectile class that wasn't described in our original diagrams, we need to comprehend first how the projectile will be attained.

The player in this instance will attain the projectile by the means of a pickup, so the player will touch or fly over the item and then the pickup/power-up will be assigned to the player. That hints to us that we shall need a pickup class as well. Let's start with that. We shall skip in making the additional UMLs for now. But it is still a really good practice to update it with our latest features. This will serve as a good source of documentation for new team members and your future self.

© Oscar Lodriguez 2019
O. Lodriguez, *Let's Build a Multiplayer Phaser Game*,
https://doi.org/10.1007/978-1-4842-4249-0_6

Pickup

A pickup in the gaming world includes items that a user can pickup. They are also often referred to as "power-ups," as they enhance the player's capabilities for a brief moment and then return the player back to normal.

Additional Folder Structure

We want to create a folder hierarchy that encapsulates our features like we understand them in our game. This is not by any means the only structure but it will help distinguish, before even writing code, what type of hierarchy you will have in your implementations. Head into the src directory.

Let's go ahead and create the following folder structure to give our feature a bit more shape and existence:

- client

  - props

    - powers

      - pickup

      - projectile

Inside the powers folder, we can create the two classes. The file "pickup.class.ts" should be in the pickup folder, and the file "projectile. class.ts" should be in the projectile folder.

- pickup

  - pickup.class.ts

- projectile

  - projectile.class.ts

We shall be leaving the projectile class empty for now. Inside of the pickup.class.ts file, let's implement the following:

Listing 6-1. src/client/props/powers/pickup/pickup.class.ts

```
export class Pickup {
        // We shall need the item we would want to be able to
        pickup. This
        // Item will have to be accessible to other classes as
        well, so we shall
        // mark it as public
        public item: Phaser.Sprite;

        constructor(game, coors) {
                // When generating the pickup, we want to pass two
                arguments. One
                // being the game instance we have created with
                Phaser. This is
                // needed to place the item into the phaser world
                this.item = game.add.sprite(coors.x, coors.y,
                'pickup');

                // Since players can pick up the pickup item in
                the game. We will
                // add physics to the object, to detect if any
                other Phaser
                // objects have collided or overlapped with this
                one pickup
                game.physics.enable(this.item, Phaser.Physics.
                ARCADE);
        }

}
```

Voila, now we need to assign items that can be picked up. I was thinking something simple, like a laser that just shoots straight. Also, it would have an ammunition count. So if the user runs out of ammo, they would need to pick it up again. Next, we need to populate our projectile class with functionality so it works as intended. The code section in Listing 6-2 will provide the code in detail.

Listing 6-2. src/client/props/powers/projectile/projectile.class.ts

```
import {Pickup} from '../pickup/pickup.class';

export class Projectile {
        // member variables
        // We can make use of Phaser's built-in weapons feature
        to keep count
        // and aim direction based on our ship's sprite
        public weapon: Phaser.Weapon;

        // Keeping the current count of the players ammunition
        public bulletCount: number;

        // Since we need to remove the pickup item from the game
        area once the
        // user has picked it up, we need a reference to the
        projectile sprite
        // item
        public pickup: Pickup;

        // To pass the projectile to the right user, we then
        also need a
        // reference of this user in our projectile class
        private player: Phaser.Sprite;

        // also let's go ahead and keep a reference of the game
        instance as well
```

```
// as we might need to directly populate our world with
the sprite
// graphic
private gameInstance: Phaser.Game;

public constructor(gameInstance, player?) {
// we will be needing to reference the game and the
player we are
// attaching the weapon on
}

public fireWeapon() {
        // one other requirement is to able to shoot and
        rid the galaxy of
        // fowl enemies!
}

public renderPickup(coors): void {
        // last but not least we need to let the
        projectile class have
        // its own graphic
        // apart from being a pickup. This way the player
        can visually see
        // which pickup they are picking up and if they
        want it or not
    }

}
```

That is a good start, we know the private and public members of the class. That makes it a lot easier for us to now populate the class with our shooting projectile mechanics.

Listing 6-3. src/client/props/powers/projectile/projectile.class.ts

```
...
// add a default bullet number you would like a pickup to
contain
// distribute. Make it a believable and fair number as games
can be very
// hard to balance correctly.
public bulletCount: number = 10;

public constructor(private gameInstance: Phaser.Game, player?) {
        // using the built-in weapon manager from Phaser, assign
        it to the
        // weapon member and add the following properties.
        this.weapon = this.gameInstance.add.weapon(10, 'laser');
        this.weapon.fireLimit = this.bulletCount;
        this.weapon.fireRate = 1000;

        // next we do a bit of defensive programming to detect
        if there is a
        // player in the constructor
        // we will understand soon why this is necessary, but it
        // boils down to projectiles existing if a player exists.
        if (player) {
                this.player = player;
                this.weapon.trackSprite(this.player, 10, 0, true);

        }
}

public fireWeapon() {
        // release the cannons!
        this.weapon.fire();
```

```
    // here we shall update out bullet count after we have
    fired
    this.bulletCount = this.weapon.fireLimit - this.weapon.
    shots;
}

public renderPickup(): void {
    // let's render our projectile as a pickup to display it
    on the screen.
    this.pickup = new Pickup(this.gameInstance, {x: 12, y: 12});
}
...
```

Our final implementation of our Projectile class should reflect the code shown in Listing 6-4.

Listing 6-4. src/client/props/powers/projectile/projectile.class.ts

```
import {Pickup} from '../pickup/pickup.class';

export class Projectile {
    public weapon: Phaser.Weapon;
    public bulletCount: number = 10;
    public pickup: Pickup;
    private player: Phaser.Sprite;

    public constructor(private gameInstance: Phaser.Game,
    player?) {
        this.weapon = this.gameInstance.add.weapon(10, 'laser');
        this.weapon.fireLimit = this.bulletCount;
        this.weapon.fireRate = 1000;
        if (player) {
            this.player = player;
            this.weapon.trackSprite(this.player, 10, 0, true);
```

```
        }
    }

    public fireWeapon() {
        this.weapon.fire();
        this.bulletCount = this.weapon.fireLimit - this.weapon.
        shots;
    }

    public renderPickup(): void {
        this.pickup = new Pickup(this.gameInstance, {x: 12,
        y: 12});
    }

}
```

Making it to the Big Screen

We are missing one small piece of the puzzle so far—that is, when do we render the pickup on the screen and to what frequency? To see results quickly we shall be sending the coordinates directly on the client side when we instantiate our projectile class. Let's refresh our memories.

All of the game logic will be in the game.ts file. This means that all of the modules come together with business rules inside of one area. This makes it easy to see what the rules of the games are.

For a much bigger project it is best to exclude the implementation and avoid having everything in one giant file. This also means possibly having the class and the implementation of the game rules on the same directory but in separate files.

We shall be doing this in our final chapter when we refactor the lot. For now let's keep it simple and implement it directly without any abstractions. Inside of game.class.ts file we will add the code from Listing 6-5.

Listing 6-5. src/client/game/game.class.ts

```
...
protected manageAssets(game): void {
        this.actors = [];
        this.actor = new Player(game);

        // create a new instance for our projectile which will
        render the pickup
        // graphic as well. We went for a composition approach
        const projectile = new Projectile(game);

        // after the instance has been created, just add water :)
        projectile.renderPickup();
...
```

By adding the new projectile and having control when and where it renders, we can place a graphic illustrating the type of power pickup the player can eventually pickup. We still have a long way to go. We are missing four fundamental features at the moment.

The first missing fundamental is the player having the ability to pickup the power. This means we should modify the player class with an assign pickup method. The second fundamental is a way to tell the game engine that the player and the pickup have overlapped with each other and to go ahead and assign the pickup to the player who was lucky enough to get ammo.

Third, we need to update our keyboard class to allow the user to fire her cannons while pressing the space bar on the keyboard. The final fundamental is adding some sort of graphic that the player has picked up the power up. We shall solve this by implementing a HUD.

The HUD will also show the total number of ammo and the remaining ammo if the player decides to unleash her cannons. We shall solve the first one pretty easily thanks to Phaser. Perform this operation with an overlap method that we shall call during the game loop.

Overlap

Phaser's overlap component, as it is referred to in the documentation, allows a game objects to validate if it overlaps with the bounds of any other game world objects.

Phaser offers an extremely handy feature to detect when objects in our game world have overlapped. We shall be using the colliding feature as well, but for the pickup in particular. We need the overlapping functionality.

Gimme the Gun!

Add a new method, assignPickup, to our player.class.ts file. It should reflect the code in Listing 6-6.

Listing 6-6. src/client/actors/player/player.class.ts

```
// import the projectile class
import {Projectile} from '../../props/powers/projectile/
projectile.class';

export class Player {
      public player: Phaser.Sprite;
      public controls: KeyBoardControl;
      public playerState: Map;
      public angularVelocity: number = 300;
      public projectile: Projectile;

      constructor(private gameInstance: Phaser.Game,
              public playerInstance: any) {
          // the playerInstance type will be picked up by a
          future section
          this.createPlayer(this.gameInstance);
```

```
        this.playerState = new Map();
}

public createPlayer(gameInstance): void {
        this.addControls();
        this.player = gameInstance.add.sprite(
            100,
            100,
            'shooter-sprite'
        );

        this.player.id = '1';
        this.player.anchor.setTo(0.5, 0.5);
        this.player.animations.add('accelerating', [1, 0],
        60, false); 26
        this.player.name = "Your name";
        this.attachPhysics(gameInstance);
}

public assignPickup(game, player?): void {
        // create a new instance of the projectile and
        assign it
        // immediately  to the player who has picked up
        the projectile
        this.projectile = new Projectile(game, player.
        player);

        // update the player state indicating that the
        player has ammo in
        // her possession, let's set the ammo to the
        projectile's default
        // bullet count to make the source of truth at
        one place
```

```
        this.playerState.set('ammo', this.projectile.
        bulletCount);
}

public view(): void {
        this.controls.update()
}

private addControls(): void {
        this.controls = new KeyBoardControl(this.
        gameInstance, this);
}

private attachPhysics(gameInstance): void {
        gameInstance.physics.enable(this.player, Phaser.
        Physics.ARCADE);
        this.player.body.collideWorldBounds = true;
        this.player.body.bounce.setTo(10, 10);
        this.player.body.gravity.y = 0;
        this.player.body.drag.set(80);
        this.player.body.maxVelocity.set(100);
        this.player.body.immovable = false;
}

}
```

Updating the Game

There needs to be a way we can tell Phaser that we have collision enabled in our gaming world for it to act on it. The following update to our game. class.ts file will make sure this is possible (see Listing 6-7).

Listing 6-7. src/client/game/game.class.ts

```
import {Player} from '../actors/player/player.class';
import {Projectile} from '../props/powers/projectile/
projectile.class';

declare const window: any;

export class Game {
      private actors: Array;
      private actor: Player;

      // promote the const to a member variable to be used
      anywhere inside of
      // our game class
      private projectile: Projectile;

      protected manageAssets(game): void {
            this.actors = [];
            this.actor = new Player(game, {x: 20, y:20});

            // change the const to a member variable so we can
            access it
            // everywhere within the Game class
            this.projectile = new Projectile(game);
            this.projectile.renderPickup();
      }

      protected gameUpdate(game): void {

            if (this.actor && this.actor.controls) {
                  this.actor.view();

                  // check if there is a projectile in the
                  game-world first
```

```
                    // or the runtime compiler will crash
                    because it is not
                    // synced with our 60fps game render
                    if (this.projectile) {

                            // implement the overlap check
                            game.physics.arcade.overlap(
                                    this.projectile.pickup.item,
                                    this.actor.player,
                                    (pickup, actor) => {
                                            // once collided.
                                            // Assign a projectile
                                            pickup
                                            // to our actor
                                            this.actor.assignPickup(
                                                    game, this.actor
                                            );
                                            pickup.kill();
                                    }
                            );
                    }

            }

    }

    protected properties(game): void {
            game.stage.disableVisibilityChange = true;
            game.add.tileSprite(0, 0, game.width, game.height,
            'space');
            game.add.sprite(0, 0, 'space');
            game.time.desiredFps = 60;
```

```
        game.renderer.clearBeforeRender = false;
        game.physics.startSystem(Phaser.Physics.ARCADE);
    }

}
```

Match up your implementation with this one to reflect the latest changes. This will ensure our game world is listening for collisions. Next we need to update our keyboard to let the game know when we want to fire a projectile.

Updating the Keyboard with a Fire!

Our keyboard needs a way to communicate with our ship. Let's implement that next (see Listing 6-8).

Listing 6-8. src/client/controls/keyboard.class.ts

```
import {Player} from '../actors/player/player.class';
import {Controls} from './keyboard.model';

export class KeyBoardControl {
    public gameControls: Controls;
    constructor(private gameInstance: any, private
    playerInstance: Player) {
        const space = Phaser.KeyCode.SPACEBAR;
        this.gameControls = {
            cursors:
                this.gameInstance.input.keyboard.
                createCursorKeys(),
            fireWeapon: this.gameInstance.input.
            keyboard.addKey(space)
        }
```

```
    }

    public update(): void {

        if (this.playerInstance.player.alive) {
            this.playerInstance.playerState.set('fire',
            false);
            const vel = this.playerInstance.
            angularVelocity;
            if (this.gameControls.cursors.up.isDown) {
            this.gameInstance.physics.arcade.
            accelerationFromRotation(
                    this.playerInstance.player.rotation,
                    100,
                    this.playerInstance.player.body.
                    acceleration);

                    this.playerInstance.player.animations
                        .play('accelerating');
                    this.playerInstance.playerState.
                    set('moving', true);
            } else {
                this.playerInstance.player.body.
                acceleration.set(0);
                this.playerInstance.playerState.
                set('moving', false);
            }

            if (this.gameControls.cursors.left.isDown) {
                this.playerInstance.player.body.
                angularVelocity = -vel;
            } else if (this.gameControls.cursors.right.
            isDown) {
```

```
            this.playerInstance.player.body.
            angularVelocity = vel;
        } else {
            this.playerInstance.player.body.
            angularVelocity = 0;
        }

        // add the ability to shoot
        if (this.gameControls.fireWeapon.isDown) {
            if (this.playerInstance.projectile) {
                // use the projectile class to
                fire the weapon
                // and update it's internal ammo
                count
                this.playerInstance.projectile.
                fireWeapon();

                // update the player state to
                firing, this will
                // be used as a hook in the near
                future for our
                // multiplayer game
                this.playerInstance.playerState
                    .set('fire', true);

            // update the bullet count in the
            player
                this.playerInstance.playerState.
                set('ammo',
                        this.playerInstance.
                        projectile.bulletCount);
            } else {
```

```
                              // update the fire map to false
                              when the user has
                              // finished firing
                              this.playerInstance.playerState
                                  .set('fire', false);
                          }

                  }

            }

        }

}
```

The HUD

One more thing is we need to do something for the HUD. The HUD, you ask...? That is game terminology for a heads up display. It is a graphical interface that games can implement to display information regarding the player in the game or the game status. The main key for the HUD is to have information available without the user having to look away from a specific focal point. If you are interested in learning more about how a HUD came about in interfaces, read the wiki page (https://en.wikipedia.org/wiki/Head-up_display).

We shall build the much-needed HUD to represent the user's current ammunition and possibly the user name as well. Create a new directory under the src/client/hud and then create another file called hud.class.ts. The HUD will then have the properties in Listing 6-9.

Listing 6-9. src/client/hud/hud.class.ts

```typescript
export class Hud {

    // will be used to display visually the current state of
    the ammo count
    private ammo: Phaser.Text;

    // we will add a feature where the user will be able to
    add her name
    private name: string;

    // since we are in outer space, we need readable text.
    here we are
    // declaring a type of font and the color it will have
    private style: { font, fill };

    constructor() {
        // declare the style to be used in the name and
        ammo text
        this.style = {
            font: '10px Arial',
            fill: '#ffffff'
        }
    }
}

// Once the user has entered their name, we can grab that value
and add
// the text to the player they have just created
public setName(game, player): void {
    this.name = game.add.text(0, 10,
        player.name.substring(0, 6),
        this.style
    );
```

```
        player.addChild(this.name);
  }

// the update method will be used as a hook that will keep
rendering the
        // initial ammo count
        public update(ammo): void {
                this.ammo.setText(`${ammo ? ammo : "}`);
        }

        // an api is handy if we want to assign ammo to a weapon
        and a player.
        // We shall be making use of this method when the user
        picks up the
        // projectile
        public setAmmo(game, player, weapon): void {
                if (this.ammo) {
                    this.ammo.setText(");
                }

                this.ammo = game.add.text(0, 25, weapon.
                bulletCount, this.style);
                player.addChild(this.ammo);

        }

}
```

Once we have the initial implementation in place, we need to implement the HUD class inside of the player class. This allows the player to make use of her name and ammo count to display through the HUD. Inside of our player class we shall update Listing 6-10.

Listing 6-10. src/client/actors/player/player.class.ts

```
import {KeyBoardControl} from '../../controls/keyboard.class';
import {Projectile} from '../../props/powers/projectile/
projectile.class';
// import the Hud class to be used inside of player
import {Hud} from '../../hud/hud.class';

export class Player {
        public player: Phaser.Sprite;
        public controls: KeyBoardControl;
        public playerState: Map;
        public angularVelocity: number = 300;

        // make the Hud public so we can access its APIs outside
        of the player
        // encapsulation
        public hud: Hud;
        public projectile: Projectile;

        constructor(private gameInstance: Phaser.Game,
                    public playerInstance: any) {
        ...
        }

        public createPlayer(gameInstance): void {
                // every player needs a Hud. This way we assign a
                hud directly to
                // the player and have access to read and writing
                text for this
                // player
                this.hud = new Hud();
```

```
                // will have the value of 'your name' We shall
                build the real name
                // functionality after we make the hud work
                this.hud.setName(gameInstance, this.player);
                ...
        }

        public assignPickup(game, player?): void {
                this.projectile = new Projectile(game, player.
                player);
                this.playerState.set('ammo', this.projectile.
                bulletCount);

                // when the user picks up an ammo, we shall want
                to update the hud
                // through the api we have created.
                this.hud.setAmmo(game, player.player, this.
                projectile);
        }

        public view(): void {
                this.controls.update();

                // always check first if we have a projectile
                instance on
                // the player or we shall get a nasty null pointer
                if (this.projectile) {
                        // take advantage of the game-loop to update
                        the ammo
                        // count if the player has been using her
                        projectiles

                        this.hud.update(this.playerState.
                        get('ammo'));
```

```
        }
    }
    ...
}
```

The final class with everything together should look like Listing 6-11.

Listing 6-11. src/client/actors/player/player.class.ts

```typescript
import {KeyBoardControl} from '../../controls/keyboard.class';
import {Projectile} from '../../props/powers/projectile/
projectile.class';
import {Hud} from '../../hud/hud.class';

export class Player {
    public player: Phaser.Sprite;
    public projectile: Projectile;
    public controls: KeyBoardControl;
    public playerState: Map<string, boolean | number>;
    public hud: Hud;
    public angularVelocity: number = 300;

    constructor(private gameInstance: Phaser.Game, public
    playerInstance: any) {
        this.createPlayer(this.gameInstance);
        this.playerState = new Map();
    }

    public createPlayer(gameInstance): void {
        this.hud = new Hud();
        this.addControls();
        this.player = gameInstance.add.sprite(
            this.playerInstance.x,
            this.playerInstance.y,
            'shooter-sprite'
```

```
    );
    this.player.id = '1';
    this.player.anchor.setTo(0.5, 0.5);
    this.player.animations.add('accelerating', [1, 0], 60,
    false);

    // will show up as 'your n' because of our name
    shortener function
    // found in the hud class
    this.player.name = 'your name';

    this.attachPhysics(gameInstance);
    this.hud.setName(gameInstance, this.player);
}

public assignPickup(game, player?): void {
    this.projectile = new Projectile(game, player.player);
    this.hud.setAmmo(game, player.player, this.projectile);
    this.playerState.set('ammo', this.projectile.bulletCount);
}

public view(): void {
    this.controls.update();
    if (this.projectile) {
        this.hud.update(this.playerState.get('ammo'));
    }
}

private addControls(): void {
    this.controls = new KeyBoardControl(this.gameInstance,
    this);
}
```

```
private attachPhysics(gameInstance): void {
    gameInstance.physics.enable(this.player, Phaser.
    Physics.ARCADE);
    this.player.body.collideWorldBounds = true;
    this.player.body.bounce.setTo(10, 10);
    this.player.body.gravity.y = 0;
    this.player.body.drag.set(80);
    this.player.body.maxVelocity.set(100);
    this.player.body.immovable = false;
  }
}
```

Conclusion

We need things to shoot at, though. Follow me in the next chapter as we explore the server side and discover how we shall be adding more spaceships in the galaxy.

CHAPTER 7

Hooking Up Our Server

In this chapter, we shall be discussing how we are going to set up the server along with socket communication as our internet protocol between the server and client. We will then create and register the player through the server and generate pickups/power-ups with random coordinates for the player to pick up.

Code for this chapter is found on GitHub (`https://github.com/codeOwl/Multiplayer-Phaser-game/tree/chapter/6`). We have come a long way space marine! I am afraid we are just halfway through our long journey.

On to the Server Side of Things!

Luckily for us, the server is a place where we can use a fairly clean and straightforward implementation without a heavy use of frameworks and libraries. Our implementation is so small, we can arguably keep everything in one file for simplicity. However, I highly encourage you to create modules if you use this project as a base for your other projects!

© Oscar Lodriguez 2019
O. Lodriguez, *Let's Build a Multiplayer Phaser Game*,
https://doi.org/10.1007/978-1-4842-4249-0_7

Models and Events

Models

Correctly configuring our application by setting up our events and models from the start saves us a lot of pain down the road by saving us time from refactoring and reimplementing our logic. Create a new folder and file inside of our src directory and call it shared. We can name the file models.ts.

```
// our spaceship model
export interface SpaceShip {
        // we need a name
        name: string;

        // a way of identifying our vessel
        id: string;

        // x- and y-coordinates we shall be receiving from the
        backend
        x: number;
        y: number;

        // the current amount of ammo the player has
        ammo: number; 15
}
```

Events

For our events, we shall be doing the same. Inside of the shared folder located in src, let's add a file called events.model.ts to encapsulate our events model. The reason we need an events model is to create the types of events we shall be using and where those events originate from. Are they from the player, game, or the server? This file will keep track of these constants so we can use them freely in our server and client-side code.

Listing 7-1. src/shared/events.model.ts

```typescript
// Events produced by our game
export class GameEvent {
        // When someone logs in successfully
        public static authentication: string =
        'authentication:successful';

        // When the game is over
        public static end: 'game:over';

        // When the game started
        public static start: 'game:start';

        // When a pickup or power-up has entered the arena
        public static drop: string = 'drop';
}

// Events produced by the Server
export class ServerEvent {
    public static connected: string = 'connection';
    public static disconnected: string = 'disconnect';
}

// Events produced by the player
export class PlayerEvent {

        // When a enemy joins
        public static joined: string = 'player:joined';

        // When the main character joins
        public static protagonist: string = 'player:protagonist';

        // When we ping all players
        public static players: string = 'actors:collection';
```

```
    // When a player dies or leaves
    public static quit: string = 'player:left';

    // When a player picks up the loot
    public static pickup: string = 'player:pickup';

    // When one gets hit
    public static hit: string = 'player:hit';

    // When the player moves we need to update the coordinates
    public static coordinates: string = 'player:coordinates';

}
```

Setting up Our Static File Server

Inside of our src directory, create a folder called server. After that, create a file with the name server.ts. We shall begin by first integrating express.js into our application. Doing so will run the server. The server then can serve our static files to the client. You can read more about express.js on their website (http://expressjs.com). We shall cover a subset of functionality but it is always nice to know what the framework is capable of.

Listing 7-2. src/server/server.ts

```
// Express.js needs the following imports to work correctly. It
is also
// appointed in the order at which it needs the imports to be
declared.
const express = require('express');
const app = express();
const http = require('http').Server(app);
```

```
// We definitely need a static file server. The fileserver's sole
// responsibility is to serve the public directory we have in
our project.
// The public server will be the artefact of our project.
Everything we
// create will be output in a bundled file with external images
and
// isolated in the public folder
app.use(express.static('public'));

// When the user visits our domain with no sub-domain. We shall
serve them
// our index.html file that contains the game and our login screen.
app.get('/', (req, res) => {
    res.sendfile(`./index.html`);
});

// GameServer class will be responsible to contain the logic of
our socket
// implementation.
class GameServer {

    // The first and necessary public method we shall need is
    a way to
    // connect to a port. Here we are keeping it simple and
    using Express'
    // easy http.listen method.
    public connect(port) {
        http.listen(port, () => {
            console.info(`Listening on port ${port}`);
        });
    }
}
```

```
// create a new instance of our game server
const gameSession = new GameServer();

// then run the connect method with any port of your choosing.
gameSession.connect(3000);
```

Socket Connection

The WebSocket protocol we are going to use allows us to interact between a web client and a web server with lower overheads, in the process paving the way for real-time data transfer bidirectionally to and from our server.

We can go on and fill out our server code with how to handle multiplayer functionality. We shall complete the entire server code in small digestible segments so we can move on and concentrate on a simple login screen. This will allow the user to login and display their names under their corresponding spaceships!

Listing 7-3. src/server/server.ts

```
import {GameEvent, PlayerEvent, ServerEvent} from './../shared/
events.model';
import {SpaceShip} from '../shared/models';
import Socket = SocketIO.Socket;
const express = require('express');
const app = express();
const http = require('http').Server(app);
const io = require('socket.io')(http);
const uuid = require('uuid');

app.use(express.static('public'));

app.get('/', (req, res) => {
    res.sendfile(`./index.html`);
});
```

```
class GameServer {

    public connect(port) {
        http.listen(port, () => {
            console.info(`Listening on port ${port}`);
        });
    }

    constructor() {
        // once we have initialized we shall call the
        socket in to start
        // listening to our events that we have yet have
        to create
        this.socketEvents();
    }

    private socketEvents() {
        // called by our class constructor. We shall
        leverage this as the
        // sole place to call all of our events. It is
        nothing more than an
        // indirection for our event's functionality with
        a socket layer.
        // Here we are declaring that if the client is
        connected to the
        // port we are listening on. We want socket To
        fire off a
        // connected event
        io.on(ServerEvent.connected, socket => {
            this.attachListeners(socket);
        });
    }
```

```
        private attachListeners(socket) {
                // Attach other events that we are interested in
                once we know a
                // user is connected to the assigned port
        }

}

const gameSession = new GameServer();

gameSession.connect(3000);
```

Next, we will implement the event handlers (see Listing 7-4).

Listing 7-4. src/server/server.ts

```
import {GameEvent, PlayerEvent, ServerEvent} from './../shared/
events.model';
import {SpaceShip} from '../shared/models';
import Socket = SocketIO.Socket;
const express = require('express');
const app = express();
const http = require('http').Server(app);
const io = require('socket.io')(http);
const uuid = require('uuid');

app.use(express.static('public'));

app.get('/', (req, res) => {
      res.sendfile(`./index.html`);
});
```

```
class GameServer {

    private dirtyFlag: boolean = false;
    constructor() {
        this.socketEvents();
    }

    public connect(port) {
        http.listen(port, () => {
            console.info(`Listening on port ${port}`);
        });
    }

    private socketEvents() {
        io.on(ServerEvent.connected, socket => {
            this.attachListeners(socket);
        });
    }

    private attachListeners(socket) {
        // Create methods corresponding to our listener class
        this.addSignOnListener(socket);
        this.addMovementListener(socket);
        this.addSignOutListener(socket);
        this.addHitListener(socket);
        this.addPickupListener(socket);
    }

    private addHitListener(socket): void {
        // called when a player gets hit
    }

    private addPickupListener(socket): void {
        // called when loot is picked up
    }
```

```
    private addMovementListener(socket): void {
        // called when player moves
    }

    private addSignOutListener(socket): void {
        // called when user quits or dies
    }

    private addSignOnListener(socket): void {
        // called when user logs on
    }

}

const gameSession = new GameServer();

gameSession.connect(3000);
```

Our server fully implemented should reflect the information in Listing 7-5.

Listing 7-5. src/server/server.ts

```
import {GameEvent, PlayerEvent, ServerEvent} from './../shared/
events.model';
import {SpaceShip} from '../shared/models';
import Socket = SocketIO.Socket;
const express = require('express');
const app = express();
const http = require('http').Server(app);
const io = require('socket.io')(http);
const uuid = require('uuid');

app.use(express.static('public'));
```

```
app.get('/', (req, res) => {
    res.sendfile(`./index.html`);
});

class GameServer {

    // A simple Boolean to detect if the game has already been
    started
    private dirtyFlag: boolean = false;

    constructor() {
        this.socketEvents();
    }

    public connect(port) {
        http.listen(port, () => {
            console.info(`Listening on port ${port}`);
        });
    }

    private socketEvents() {
        io.on(ServerEvent.connected, socket => {
            this.attachListeners(socket);
        });
    }

    private attachListeners(socket) {
        this.addSignOnListener(socket);
        this.addMovementListener(socket);
        this.addSignOutListener(socket);
        this.addHitListener(socket);
        this.addPickupListener(socket);
    }
```

```
private addHitListener(socket) {
    // If the player has been hit, we get a player hit
    event, including the
    // player id, notifying the others that this specific
    player has
    // been struck
    socket.on(PlayerEvent.hit, (playerId) => {
        socket.broadcast.emit(PlayerEvent.hit, playerId);
    });
}

private gameInitialized(socket): void {
    // initialize the game if the first user logs in
    if (!this.dirtyFlag) {
        this.dirtyFlag = true;

        // Generate pickup loot every 10 seconds so the
        players can
        // replenish their ammo
        setInterval(() => {
            const coordinates = {x: Math.floor(Math.
            random() * 1024) + 1, y: Math.floor(Math.
            random() * 768) + 1};
            socket.emit(GameEvent.drop, coordinates);
            socket.broadcast.emit(GameEvent.drop,
            coordinates);
        }, 10000);
    }
}
```

```
private addPickupListener(socket) {

    // If the player picks up an item. Emit the pickup
    event to notify
    // the front end
    socket.on(PlayerEvent.pickup, (player) => {
        socket.player.ammo = player.ammo;
        socket.broadcast.emit(PlayerEvent.pickup,
        player.uuid);
    });
}

private addMovementListener(socket) {
    // Keep track of the player positions
    socket.on(PlayerEvent.coordinates, (coors) => {
        socket.broadcast.emit(PlayerEvent.coordinates,
        {coors: coors, player: socket.player});
    });
}

private addSignOutListener(socket): void {
    // Detect if a player has died or has quit the session
    socket.on(ServerEvent.disconnected, () => {
        if (socket.player) {
            socket.broadcast.emit(PlayerEvent.quit,
            socket.player.id);
        }
    });
}
```

```
private addSignOnListener(socket): void {
    // Detect if a player has joined the session
    socket.on(GameEvent.authentication, (player, gameSize)
    => {
        socket.emit(PlayerEvent.players, this.
        getAllPlayers());
        this.createPlayer(socket, player, gameSize);
        socket.emit(PlayerEvent.protagonist,
        socket.player);
        socket.broadcast.emit(PlayerEvent.joined,
        socket.player);
        this.gameInitialized(socket);
    });
}

private createPlayer(socket, player: SpaceShip,
    windowSize: { x, y }): void {
    // here is where the magic happens. We create a new
    player and add
    // the following properties to her
    socket.player = {
        name: player.name,
        id: uuid(),
        ammo: 0,
        x: this.randomInt(0, windowSize.x),
        y: this.randomInt(0, windowSize.y)
    };
}

private get players(): number {
    // a method for collecting the total player length
    return Object.keys(io.sockets.connected).length;
}
```

```
    private getAllPlayers(): Array<SpaceShip> {
        // We need a way to notify all of the players. Using
        this method we
        // can always get all of the current players logged
        into our session
        const players = [];
        Object.keys(io.sockets.connected).map((socketID) => {
            const player = io.sockets.connected[socketID].
            player;
            if (player) {
                players.push(player);
            }
        });
        return players;
    }

    private randomInt(low, high) {
        // for generating random coordinates, we shall be using
        this one a
        // lot as we are generating both random coordinates for
        our players
        // and our loot
        return Math.floor(Math.random() * (high - low) + low);
    }
}

const gameSession = new GameServer();

gameSession.connect(3000);
```

Back to the Client

This, of course, bakes in a lot of new functionality that our game can muster. Let's head back and update our initial game file located on the client side.

Listing 7-6. src/client/game/game.ts

```
import {Player} from '../actors/player/player.class';
import {Projectile} from '../props/powers/projectile/
projectile.class';
// import our created events
import {GameEvent, PlayerEvent} from '../../shared/events.
model';

declare const window: any;

export class Game {
    private actors: Array<Player>;
    private actor: Player;
    private projectile: Projectile;

    // create a new socket io session
    constructor() {
        window.socket = io.connect();
    }

    protected manageAssets(game): void {
        this.actors = [];

        // Once the server has detected that a new player has
        joined we
        // shall notify our client to create a new player for
        us on
```

```
window.socket.on(PlayerEvent.joined, (player) => {
    this.actors.push(new Player(game, player));
});

// Once you have joined (the protagonist) we need a
special event
// for you. This so we can determine that you are the
main player in
// your world and the others are your enemy
window.socket.on(PlayerEvent.protagonist, (player) => {
    this.actor = new Player(game, player);
    this.actors.push(this.actor);
});

window.socket.on(PlayerEvent.players, (players) => {
    // If a new player or a returning player joins our
    game. We
    // shall collect all of the players and their
    current states and
    // update their clients with the data. This way
    what he is
    // seeing is not any different to what others are
    seeing
    players.map((player: any) => {
        const enemy = new Player(game, player);
        if (player.ammo) {
            enemy.assignPickup(game, enemy);
        }
        this.actors.push(enemy);
    });
});
```

```
window.socket.on(PlayerEvent.quit, (playerId) => {
    // If a player dies or quits, we call the following
    actions on
    // the actors array.
    // First we filter who quit or died and then move
    to removing
    // them from the game world
    this.actors
        .filter(actor => actor.player.id === playerId)
        .map(actor => actor.player.body.sprite.destroy());
});

window.socket.on(GameEvent.drop, (coors) => {
    // our server will be causing a loot drop every 10
    seconds. When
    // this happens we want to act upon it.

    // if there is already a loot in our world, we
    shall remove it
    // before placing the new one.
    if (this.projectile) {
        this.projectile.pickup.item.kill();
    }

    // create a new loot every 10 seconds and pass the
    coordinates
    // sent by the server
    this.projectile = new Projectile(game);
    this.projectile.renderPickup(coors);
});
```

```
window.socket.on(PlayerEvent.hit, (enemy) => {
    // similar to when a player quits we detect who the
    player was
    // and reload their client so they get brought back
    into the
    // game to try again if they dare face you again!
    this.actors
        .filter(actor => this.actor.player.id === enemy)
        .map(actor => window.location.reload());
});

window.socket.on(PlayerEvent.pickup, (player) => {
    // Once the projectile has been picked up, we shall
    assign it to
    // the user that has picked it up
    this.actors
        .filter(actor => actor.player.id === player)
        .map(actor => actor.assignPickup(game, actor));

    // kill the pick for the other players as well
    this.projectile.pickup.item.kill();
});

window.socket.on(PlayerEvent.coordinates, (player) => {
    // This is the heart of our multiplayer game.
    Because here we
    // decided to keep track of all of the other
    players actions in
    // our gameworld, if a new player joins, he or she
    needs to be
    // aware of who is already in the game world and
    what their ammo
```

```
        // levels are. We in the industry call this the
        current state.
        this.actors.filter((actor: Player) => {
            if (actor.player.id === player.player.id) {
                actor.player.x = player.coors.x;
                actor.player.y = player.coors.y;
                actor.player.rotation = player.coors.r;

                // Update the player hud
                if (actor.projectile) {
                    actor.hud.update(player.coors.a);
                }

                // detect if the player is shooting
                if (player.coors.f) {
                    actor.projectile.fireWeapon();
                }

                if (player.coors.m) {
                    // if the enemy player is moving, we
                    shall add the
                    // moving animation to their ship. This
                    way in our
                    // screen we do not see him moving
                    about without any
                    // thrusters!
                    actor.player.animations.
                    play('accelerating');
                }
            }
        });
    });
}
```

```
protected gameUpdate(game): void {
    // This method is called through the Phaser engine
    class we
    // created before. This means that it is running an
    endless loop to
    // update in real time what the characters are up to.
    Someone needs
    // to keep an eye on them!
    if (this.actor && this.actor.controls) {
        this.actor.view();

        // During the loop we shall constantly be emitting
        the state of
        // our player. Once we have a change in our
        coordinates or if we
        // are firing, a new event is triggered which will
        in turn notify
        // the server whom will notify the other connected
        clients
        window.socket.emit(PlayerEvent.coordinates, {
            x: this.actor.player.position.x,
            y: this.actor.player.position.y,
            r: this.actor.player.rotation,
            f: this.actor.playerState.get('fire'),
            m: this.actor.playerState.get('moving'),
            a: this.actor.playerState.get('ammo')
        });

        // In the loop we shall also check if the player
        collides with
        // another player. If they do, we shall make the
        arcade engine
```

```
// do it's default action, which is to let them
bounce off of
// each other because of the player properties we
added when
// creating the player
game.physics.arcade.collide(
    this.actor.player,
    this.actors.map(actor => actor.player)
);

// If the bullet collides with a player, we need a
way to
// tell both the player and the bullet to destroy
themselves.
// Here we are matching whether if the fired bullet
collided with an
// enemy based on the id of that enemy. If so
destroy both
// sprites. Once destroyed they will notify the
server so every
// client will be updated of the event.
if (this.actor.projectile) {
    game.physics.arcade.collide(
        this.actor.projectile.weapon.bullets,
        this.actors.map((actor) => actor.player),
        (enemy, projectile) => {
            if (enemy.id !== this.actor.player.id) {
                // make the player explode
                this.actor.projectile.
                kaboom(projectile);
                // update the server about the
                player who has
```

```
                        // been hit and pass along the id
                        window.socket.emit(PlayerEvent.hit,
                        enemy.id);

                        // destroy the sprites in the view
                        projectile.kill();
                        enemy.kill();
                    }
                }
        );
    }

// this time we shall be using the overlap to
detect if the
// player has picked up a projectile
// first we detect which player it is who has
overlapped with
// the pickup.
// then we notify all of the listeners who it was.
// lastly we destroy the pickup
if (this.projectile) {
    game.physics.arcade.overlap(this.projectile.
    pickup.item,
        this.actors.map((actor) => actor.player),
        (pickup, actor) => {
            this.actors
                .filter(actorInstance =>
                    actor.id === actorInstance.
                    player.id
                )
```

```
                              .map(actorInstance =>
                                  actorInstance.assignPickup
                                  (game, actorInstance)
                              );
                      window.socket.emit(PlayerEvent.pickup, {
                          uuid: actor.id,
                          ammo: true
                      });
                      pickup.kill();
                  });
              }
          }
      }

      protected properties(game): void {
          game.stage.disableVisibilityChange = true;
          game.add.tileSprite(0, 0, game.width, game.height,
          'space');
          game.add.sprite(0, 0, 'space');
          game.time.desiredFps = 60;
          game.renderer.clearBeforeRender = false;
          game.physics.startSystem(Phaser.Physics.ARCADE);
      }

  }
```

Marvelous Explosions!

This would mean that we have a semi-functioning game! But remember
how we wanted to kill the player and we have implemented a kaboom
method. Well the player does not have this method yet, so let's update the
player to be allowed to be destroyed in a marvelous explosion! Inside of

our props folder, create a new directory called "explosion." Inside of the newly created directory, create a file called explosion.class.ts.

Listing 7-7. src/client/props/explosion/explosion.class.ts

```
export class Explode {
        // the explosions property will be a phaser sprite
        private explosions: Phaser.Sprite;

        constructor(gameInstance, projectile) {
                // let's add the sprite and give it a graphic that
                we already have
                // in our start project called kaboom
                this.explosions = gameInstance.add.sprite(64, 64,
                'kaboom');

                // We also have an animation that will play this
                kaboom! :D
                this.explosions.animations.add('kaboom');

                // We shall need an offset to center the explosion
                on our
                //sprites
                this.explosions.reset(projectile.body.x + -20,
                                      projectile.body.y - 30);

                // Phaser offers us a play method for animations
                to be played and
                // will commence as soon as the explode class is
                created
                this.explosions.animations.play('kaboom', 15,
                false);

                // after half a second of the animation playing we
                shall
```

```
        // kill the sprite to release its burden on our
        memory
        setTimeout(() => {
                this.explosions.kill();
        }, 500);
    }
}
```

Back in our projectile class, we want to look at different usages of projectiles to determine how they impact a certain enemy or object. Implementing kaboom, which is an explosion with fire in space... hum, means that all of our ships will destroy the same way, but what if there was another projectile? Wouldn't it be awesome if that projectile had another way of killing our targets? Let's say a vaporizing ray? With that reasoning in mind, let's create the kaboom method in the projectile class (see Listing 7-8).

Listing 7-8. src/client/props/powers/projectile/projectile.class.ts

```
import {Pickup} from '../pickup/pickup.class';

export class Projectile {
    public weapon: Phaser.Weapon;
    public bulletCount: number = 10;
    public pickup: Pickup;
    private player: Phaser.Sprite;

    public constructor(private gameInstance: Phaser.Game,
    player?) {
        this.weapon = this.gameInstance.add.weapon(10,
        'laser');
        this.weapon.fireLimit = this.bulletCount;
        this.weapon.fireRate = 1000;
```

```
    if (player) {
        this.player = player;
        this.weapon.trackSprite(this.player, 10, 0, true);
    }
}

public fireWeapon() {
    this.weapon.fire();
    this.bulletCount = this.weapon.fireLimit - this.weapon.
    shots;
}

public renderPickup(): void {
    this.pickup = new Pickup(this.gameInstance,
    {x: 12, y: 12});
}

// our kaboom class is fairly short and straightforward
public kaboom(projectile) {
    // all we need is a new class instance with the
    following arguments
    new Explode(this.gameInstance, projectile);
}

}
```

Conclusion

To make our game work, we need to add one more thing. There are a lot of features we are adding quickly, but this is the last one, as it will help our user identify their spaceship on-screen! Follow me to the next section with the mission of telling the galaxy your name.

CHAPTER 8

The World Should Remember Your Name

In this chapter, we shall be discussing –the login screen for acquiring the user name. The game code for this chapter is found on GitHub (`https://github.com/codeOwl/Multiplayer-Phaser-game/tree/chapter/7`). You have rid the galaxy of foes and evil-doers, but there is no way of ever knowing your name! We are not masked crusaders, we are people and want credit where it's due dammit! We need an input field where the user can enter their name into our game, so we can save it somewhere and display it under the spaceship. Hmmm. Consider the following proposition.

Login

We build a login scene, where the user is met with an input field where she can type her name. After that, she will then be presented with the galaxy with her name right under her ship. In this final chapter, we shall be implementing such a login screen.

© Oscar Lodriguez 2019
O. Lodriguez, *Let's Build a Multiplayer Phaser Game*,
https://doi.org/10.1007/978-1-4842-4249-0_8

Listing 8-1. src/client/scenes/login.class.ts

```
// import our game event model so we can use it to notify when
the user has
// been logged into our game!
import {GameEvent} from '../../shared/events.model';

declare const window: any;

export class LoginScene {

    public formContainer: HTMLDivElement;
    public loginPage: HTMLDivElement;
    public form: HTMLDivElement;
    public loginForm: HTMLFormElement;
    public input: HTMLInputElement;
    public button: HTMLButtonElement;
    private name: any;

    constructor() {
        this.createForm()
    }

    private createForm() {
        // fairly straightforward DOM manipulation syntax for
        our form. Feel
        // free to use this one or create your own sassy form
        this.formContainer = document.createElement('div');
        this.formContainer.className = 'form-container';

        this.loginPage = document.createElement('div');
        this.loginPage.className = 'login-page';

        this.form = document.createElement('div');
        this.form.className = 'form';
```

```
    this.loginForm = document.createElement('form');

    this.input = document.createElement('input');
    this.input.setAttribute('type', 'text');
    this.input.placeholder = 'username';
    this.input.id = 'your-name';
    this.input.focus();

    this.button = document.createElement('button');
    this.button.innerText = 'Join game';
    this.button.addEventListener('click', (e) => this.
    createPlayer(e));

    this.loginForm.appendChild(this.input);
    this.loginForm.appendChild(this.button);
    this.loginPage.appendChild(this.form);
    this.form.appendChild(this.loginForm);
    this.formContainer.appendChild(this.loginPage);

    document.body.appendChild(this.formContainer);
}

private createPlayer(e): void {
    // once the player has been created. We want to remove
    the login
    // screen and show the game
    e.preventDefault();

    // remove the login screen
    this.toggleLogin();

    // save the name value the user entered
    const name = this.input.value;
```

```
        // ship the following payload to the server.
        window.socket.emit(GameEvent.authentication, {name}, {
            x: window.innerWidth,
            y: window.innerHeight
        });
    }

    // the private method called within our class that
    toggles the
    // visibility of our login form
    private toggleLogin(): void {
        this.formContainer.classList.toggle('visible');
    }

}
```

We will be implementing this login screen also in our "game.ts" file. Let's do so now! :))))

Listing 8-2. src/client/game/game.ts

```
import {Player} from '../actors/player/player.class';
import {Projectile} from '../props/powers/projectile/
projectile.class';
import {GameEvent, PlayerEvent} from '../../shared/events.
model';

declare const window: any;

export class Game {
    public login: LoginScene;
    private actors: Array<Player>;
    private actor: Player;
    private projectile: Projectile;
```

```
constructor() {
    window.socket = io.connect();
    // create the new instance for the login screen
    this.login = new LoginScene();
}
...
}
```

Since we are now rendering the pickup from the server, we need to update our projectile class as well. Instead of passing the hard object we can literally pass in the real coordinates!

Listing 8-3. src/client/props/powers/projectile/projectile.class.ts

```
import {Pickup} from '../pickup/pickup.class';

export class Projectile {
    public weapon: Phaser.Weapon;
    public bulletCount: number = 10;
    public pickup: Pickup;
    private player: Phaser.Sprite;

    public constructor(private gameInstance: Phaser.Game,
    player?) {
        this.weapon = this.gameInstance.add.weapon(10,
        'laser');
        this.weapon.fireLimit = this.bulletCount;
        this.weapon.fireRate = 1000;
        if (player) {
            this.player = player;
            this.weapon.trackSprite(this.player, 10, 0, true);
        }
    }
```

```
public fireWeapon() {
    this.weapon.fire();
    this.bulletCount = this.weapon.fireLimit - this.weapon.
    shots;
}

public renderPickup(coors): void {
    // pass in the coors we get from the server through our
    game class
    this.pickup = new Pickup(this.gameInstance, coors);
}

public kaboom(projectile) {
    new Explode(this.gameInstance, projectile);
}

}
```

While we are at it, let's update our player class to also take the real data and not the stub we created earlier.

Listing 8-4. src/client/actors/player/player.ts

```
import {KeyBoardControl} from '../../controls/keyboard.class';
import {Projectile} from '../../props/powers/projectile/
projectile.class';
import {Hud} from '../../hud/hud.class';

export class Player {
    public player: Phaser.Sprite;
    public projectile: Projectile;
    public controls: KeyBoardControl;
    public playerState: Map<string, boolean | number>;
    public hud: Hud;
    public angularVelocity: number = 300;
```

```
constructor(private gameInstance: Phaser.Game, public
playerInstance: any) {
    this.createPlayer(this.gameInstance);
    this.playerState = new Map();
}

public createPlayer(gameInstance): void {
    this.hud = new Hud();
    this.addControls();
    // update to include the playerInstance instead
    this.player = gameInstance.add.sprite(this.
    playerInstance.x, this.playerInstance.y,
    'shooter-sprite');

    // update to include the playerInstance instead
    this.player.id = this.playerInstance.id;
    this.player.anchor.setTo(0.5, 0.5);
    this.player.animations.add('accelerating', [1, 0], 60,
    false);

    // update to include the playerInstance instead
    this.player.name = this.playerInstance.name;
    this.attachPhysics(gameInstance);
    this.hud.setName(gameInstance, this.player);
}

public assignPickup(game, player?): void {
    this.projectile = new Projectile(game, player.player);
    this.hud.setAmmo(game, player.player, this.projectile);
    this.playerState.set('ammo', this.projectile.
    bulletCount);
}
```

```typescript
public view(): void {
    this.controls.update();
    if (this.projectile) {
        this.hud.update(this.playerState.get('ammo'));
    }
}

private addControls(): void {
    this.controls = new KeyBoardControl(this.gameInstance,
    this);
}

private attachPhysics(gameInstance): void {
    gameInstance.physics.enable(this.player, Phaser.
    Physics.ARCADE);
    this.player.body.collideWorldBounds = true;
    this.player.body.bounce.setTo(10, 10);
    this.player.body.gravity.y = 0;
    this.player.body.drag.set(80);
    this.player.body.maxVelocity.set(100);
    this.player.body.immovable = false;
}

}
```

It would be nice if we also added an effect when any item has entered the game world. This way we discern much easier what has been changed in our game world. Inside of our props folder, let's create a new directory called particle. Inside the new folder create a new file called "particle.class.ts".

Listing 8-5. src/client/props/particle/particle.class.ts

```
export class Particle {

    // add a member to the particle class that keeps the
    instance of the
    // phaser sprite.
    private particle: Phaser.Sprite;

    constructor(gameInstance: Phaser.Game, sprite: Phaser.
    Sprite) {
        // we already have graphic and animation waiting, so
        let's use that // one.
        this.particle = gameInstance.add.sprite(64, 64, 'dust');
        this.particle.animations.add('dust');
        this.particle.reset(sprite.body.x + -20, sprite.
        body.y - 30);
        this.particle.animations.play('dust', 16, false);

        setTimeout(() => {
            // after the animation we can just kill the sprite.
            this.particle.kill();
        }, 1000);
    }
}
```

Once the particle class is in place, we need to rationalize where and when we shall be using it. I think personally it would work well when a new player has joined the game but also when the server generates a loot drop. Your final player class will look like this:

```
import {KeyBoardControl} from '../../controls/keyboard.class';
import {Projectile} from '../../props/powers/projectile/
projectile.class';
import {Hud} from '../../hud/hud.class';
```

```typescript
import {Particle} from '../../props/particle/particle.class';

export class Player {
    public player: Phaser.Sprite;
    public projectile: Projectile;
    public controls: KeyBoardControl;
    public playerState: Map<string, boolean | number>;
    public hud: Hud;
    public angularVelocity: number = 300;
    private particle: Particle;

    constructor(private gameInstance: Phaser.Game, public
    playerInstance: any) {
        this.createPlayer(this.gameInstance);
        this.playerState = new Map();
    }

    public createPlayer(gameInstance): void {
        this.hud = new Hud();
        this.addControls();
        this.player = gameInstance.add.sprite(this.
        playerInstance.x,
            this.playerInstance.y, 'shooter-sprite');
        this.player.id = this.playerInstance.id;
        this.player.anchor.setTo(0.5, 0.5);
        this.player.animations.add('accelerating', [1, 0], 60,
        false);
        this.player.name = this.playerInstance.name;
        this.attachPhysics(gameInstance);
        this.hud.setName(gameInstance, this.player);
        this.particle = new Particle(gameInstance, this.player);
    }
```

```
public assignPickup(game, player?): void {
    this.projectile = new Projectile(game, player.player);
    this.hud.setAmmo(game, player.player, this.projectile);
    this.playerState.set('ammo', this.projectile.
    bulletCount);
}

public view(): void {
    this.controls.update();
    if (this.projectile) {
        this.hud.update(this.playerState.get('ammo'));
    }
}

private addControls(): void {
    this.controls = new KeyBoardControl(this.gameInstance,
    this);
}

private attachPhysics(gameInstance): void {
    gameInstance.physics.enable(this.player, Phaser.
    Physics.ARCADE);
    this.player.body.collideWorldBounds = true;
    this.player.body.bounce.setTo(10, 10);
    this.player.body.gravity.y = 0;
    this.player.body.drag.set(80);
    this.player.body.maxVelocity.set(100);
    this.player.body.immovable = false;
}
}
```

We now need to add the same particle implementation for both the projectile and pickup classes.

Listing 8-6. src/client/props/powers/projectile/projectile.class.ts

```ts
import {Explode} from '../../explosion/explosion.class';
import {Pickup} from '../pickup/pickup.class';
import {Particle} from '../../particle/particle.class';

export class Projectile {
    public weapon: Phaser.Weapon;
    public bulletCount: number = 10;
    public pickup: Pickup;
    private player: Phaser.Sprite;
    private gameInstance: Phaser.Game;
    private particle: Particle;

    public constructor(gameInstance, player?) {
        this.gameInstance = gameInstance;
        this.weapon = gameInstance.add.weapon(this.bulletCount,
        'laser');
        this.weapon.fireLimit = this.bulletCount;
        this.weapon.fireRate = 1000;
        if (player) {
            this.player = player;
            this.weapon.trackSprite(this.player, 10, 0, true);
        }
    }

    public fireWeapon() {
        this.weapon.fire();
        this.bulletCount = this.weapon.fireLimit - this.weapon.
        shots;
    }
```

```
public renderPickup(coors): void {
    this.pickup = new Pickup(this.gameInstance, coors);
    this.particle = new Particle(this.gameInstance, this.
    pickup.item);
}

public kaboom(projectile) {
    new Explode(this.gameInstance, projectile);
}
}
```

Do the same for the pickup class by adding the particle inside of the constructor.

Listing 8-7. src/client/props/powers/pickup/pickup.class.ts

```
import {Particle} from '../../particle/particle.class';
import * as Phaser from 'phaser-ce';

export class Pickup {

    public item: Phaser.Sprite;
    private particle: Particle;

    constructor(game, coors) {
        this.item = game.add.sprite(coors.x, coors.y, 'pickup');
        game.physics.enable(this.item, Phaser.Physics.ARCADE);
        this.particle = new Particle(game, this.item);
    }

}
```

Congratulations!

Running npm start on your initial directory will launch the game and you can play and explore by adding new features! The next chapter is all based on the Phaser community and how you may leverage it to make awesome game experiences in the near future!

CHAPTER 9

Bonus! Refactoring & Asteroids

For the diehards in us who want to learn to add another complex feature, this one is for you! In the upcoming chapter we shall learn to refactor our functionality for reusability while implementing comets on the server side. We shall also render the comets on the client side and update the player class to implement its own explode method.

Adding More Features

Let's add a new feature that adds a new level of threat to our galaxy in the form of giant asteroids. We shall be keeping our implementation fairly simple, considering complexity could increase rather quickly.

Refactoring

Refactoring is a crucial part of software engineering. The reason is we need software to work within a specific deadline, or we need to build for the features we are supporting now. After a while, we get to implement new features or enhance existing functionalities.

© Oscar Lodriguez 2019
O. Lodriguez, *Let's Build a Multiplayer Phaser Game*,
https://doi.org/10.1007/978-1-4842-4249-0_9

That's when it might dawn on us that we might want to do a bit of refactoring to make a class leaner, cleaner, or more reusable. This is the case with our explode class that is located directly in the projectile class. If a comet or a projectile hits our player, we want the ship to explode. Following this new rationalization, we can go ahead and refactor our projectile class to look like Listing 9-1.

Listing 9-1. src/client/props/powers/projectile/projectile.class.ts

```ts
import {Pickup} from '../pickup/pickup.class';
import {Particle} from '../../particle/particle.class';

export class Projectile {
    public weapon: Phaser.Weapon;
    public bulletCount: number = 10;
    public pickup: Pickup;
    private player: Phaser.Sprite;
    private gameInstance: Phaser.Game;

    public constructor(gameInstance, player?) {
        this.gameInstance = gameInstance;
        this.weapon = gameInstance.add.weapon(this.bulletCount,
        'laser');
        this.weapon.fireLimit = this.bulletCount;
        this.weapon.fireRate = 1000;
        if (player) {
            this.player = player;
            this.weapon.trackSprite(this.player, 10, 0, true);
        }
    }
```

```
    public fireWeapon() {
        this.weapon.fire();
        this.bulletCount = this.weapon.fireLimit - this.weapon.
        shots;
    }

    public renderPickup(coors): void {
        this.pickup = new Pickup(this.gameInstance, coors);
        new Particle(this.gameInstance, this.pickup.item);
    }
}
```

We moved out the kaboom method, and this will be placed inside of the player class for controlling how the player would get destroyed if such an event occurs!

Listing 9-2. src/client/actors/player/player.class.ts

```
import {KeyBoardControl} from '../../controls/keyboard.class';
import {Projectile} from '../../props/powers/projectile/
projectile.class';
import {Hud} from '../../hud/hud.class';
import {Particle} from '../../props/particle/particle.class';
import {SpaceShip} from '../../../shared/models';
import {Explode} from '../../props/explosion/explosion.class';

export class Player {
    public player: Phaser.Sprite;
    public projectile: Projectile;
    public controls: KeyBoardControl;
    public playerState: Map<string, boolean | number>;
    public hud: Hud;
    public angularVelocity: number = 300;
    private particle: Particle;
```

```
constructor(private gameInstance: Phaser.Game,
            public playerInstance: SpaceShip) {
    this.createPlayer(this.gameInstance);
    this.playerState = new Map();
}

public createPlayer(gameInstance): void {
    this.hud = new Hud();
    this.addControls();
    this.player = gameInstance.add.sprite(this.
    playerInstance.x,
        this.playerInstance.y, 'shooter-sprite');
    this.player.id = this.playerInstance.id;
    this.player.anchor.setTo(0.5, 0.5);
    this.player.animations.add('accelerating', [1, 0], 60,
    false);
    this.player.name = this.playerInstance.name;
    this.attachPhysics(gameInstance);

    // we will have a destroy method for the player that
    calls the
    // explode and kills the player for clean up afterward.
    This is
    // exactly what we want to express if the player
    happens to be
    // killed by anything
    this.player.destroy = () => {
        new Explode(this.gameInstance, this.player);
        this.player.kill();
    }

    this.hud.setName(gameInstance, this.player);
    this.particle = new Particle(gameInstance, this.player);
}
```

```typescript
    public assignPickup(game, player?): void {
        this.projectile = new Projectile(game, player.player);
        this.hud.setAmmo(game, player.player, this.projectile);
        this.playerState.set('ammo', this.projectile.bulletCount);
    }

    public view(): void {
        this.controls.update();
        if (this.projectile) {
            this.hud.update(this.playerState.get('ammo'));
        }
    }

    private addControls(): void {
        this.controls = new KeyBoardControl(this.gameInstance,
        this);
    }

    private attachPhysics(gameInstance): void {
        gameInstance.physics.enable(this.player, Phaser.
        Physics.ARCADE);
        this.player.body.collideWorldBounds = true;
        this.player.body.bounce.setTo(10, 10);
        this.player.body.gravity.y = 0;
        this.player.body.drag.set(80);
        this.player.body.maxVelocity.set(100);
        this.player.body.immovable = false;
    }

}
```

That should cover the part of our classes in terms of refactoring. We need to change our "game.class.ts" file to reflect these changes as well, or our game will just break since it has no idea we just had a refactoring occurrence.

Asteroids!

Navigate to inside of the props folder, and create the following folder called "asteroid." Inside of asteroid create a class called "astroid.class.ts".

Listing 9-3. src/client/props/asteroid/asteroid.class.ts

```
export class Asteroid {

    public asteroid: Phaser.Sprite;

    constructor(gameInstance) {
        this.asteroid = gameInstance.add.sprite(0, -128,
        'asteroid');
        this.asteroid.animations.add('asteroid');
        this.asteroid.animations.play('asteroid', 10, true,
        false);
        this.attachPhysics(gameInstance);
    }

    private attachPhysics(gameInstance): void {
        gameInstance.physics.enable(this.asteroid, Phaser.
        Physics.ARCADE);
        this.asteroid.body.collideWorldBounds = false;
        this.asteroid.body.bounce.setTo(0);
        this.asteroid.body.gravity.y = 0;
        this.asteroid.body.drag.set(80);
        this.asteroid.body.maxVelocity.set(100);
        this.asteroid.body.immovable = true;
    }
}
```

As you can see, this is not any new knowledge. We have been doing this for all the other props and other classes located throughout the project. It's an achievement to you that you already know this crucial creation process of our Phaser sprites. Once we have the class, we need to update our game. class.ts with the functionality that the asteroids will bring to the table.

Listing 9-4. src/client/game/game.class.ts

```
// ...
// import the asteroid class
import {Asteroid} from '../props/asteroid/asteroid.class';

// since our focus is not getting the Window object typed, we
can leave this as any, as it removes the overhead of typing it.
declare const window: any;

export class Game {
    // ...
    // Add a type to a null object called comet
    private comet: Asteroid;

    protected manageAssets(game): void {
        // ...
        // create a new instance of a comet to match the server
        if a new
        // player joined the room
        this.comet = new Asteroid(game);

        // Add a new method to listen to the create event from
        the server so
        // we can create and sync the asteroid field for all of
        the clients
        window.socket.on(CometEvent.create, () => {
            this.comet = new Asteroid(game);
        });
```

```
    // once the asteroid exists, we need to update its
    coordinates
    // throughout the game instance. We shall achieve that
    with this
    // method, which will get a direct feed from our server
    window.socket.on(CometEvent.coordinates, (coors) => {
        if (this.comet) {
            this.comet.asteroid.x = coors.x;
            this.comet.asteroid.y = coors.y;
        }
    });

    // lastly we add the destroy so when the asteroid is
    out of bounds,
    // we shall call this method to destroy the comet in
    order to
    // instantiate a new one
    window.socket.on(CometEvent.destroy, () => {
        if (this.comet) {
            this.comet.asteroid.kill();
            this.comet = null;
        }
    });
    // ...
}

protected gameUpdate(game): void {
    // ...

    // lastly we need to add a simple detector to see if
    the comet has
```

```
    // collided with any user along its way down the screen
    if (this.comet) {
        game.physics.arcade.collide(this.comet.asteroid,
            this.actors.map(actor => actor.player), (comet,
            actor) => {
                if (actor.id !== this.actor.player.id) {
                    // if the player hit is not our current
                    player, then
                    // emit the topic and the actor it did
                    hit for their
                    // screen to go back to login and
                    // remove all states
                    window.socket.emit(PlayerEvent.hit,
                    actor.id);
                } else {
                    // otherwise just bring us to the login
                    screen and
                    // remove all states
                    window.location.reload();
                }
            });
    }
    // ...
}
// ...

}
```

Since we are already using "comet"-specific events as topics for our subscription callback using sockets, we can go ahead and update our models to supports these constants.

Listing 9-5. src/shared/events.model.ts

```typescript
export class GameEvent {
    public static authentication: string =
    'authentication:successful';
    public static end: 'game:over';
    public static start: 'game:start';
    public static drop: string = 'drop';
}

export class CometEvent {
    public static create: string = 'comet:create';
    public static destroy: string = 'comet:destroy';
    public static coordinates: string = 'comet:coordinates';
}

export class ServerEvent {
    public static connected: string = 'connection';
    public static disconnected: string = 'disconnect';
}

export class PlayerEvent {
    public static joined: string = 'player:joined';
    public static protagonist: string = 'player:protagonist';
    public static players: string = 'actors:collection';
    public static quit: string = 'player:left';
    public static pickup: string = 'player:pickup';
    public static hit: string = 'player:hit';
    public static coordinates: string = 'player:coordinates';
}
```

The last step we should take is to update our server to make the appropriate calls.

Listing 9-6. src/server/server.ts

```
// ...
import {
    CometEvent,
    GameEvent,
    PlayerEvent,
    ServerEvent
} from './../shared/events.model';

class GameServer {
    // ...
    private gameHasStarted: boolean = false;

    // check if the comet is already in the game instance
    private hasComet: boolean = false;

    private gameInitialized(socket): void {
        if (!this.gameHasStarted) {
            this.gameHasStarted = true;
            // once the game has started for the first time,
            called the
            // create comet class which takes two arguments.
            The socket
            // instance and the interval we want to check if we
            need to add
            // a new comet/asteroid to our game
            this.createComet(socket, 1000);
            // ...
        }
    }
}
```

```
private createComet(socket, interval: number) {
    // here we have an interval that loops every 1 second
    to check if we
    // need to add a comet to our game
    setInterval(() => {
        if (!this.hasComet) {
            // if there isn't a comet, add one! Then notify
            all of the
            // channels that we have added this comet.
            Later we update
            // the comet coordinates
            this.hasComet = true;
            socket.emit(CometEvent.create);
            socket.broadcast.emit(CometEvent.create);
            this.updateComet(socket);
        }
    }, interval);
}

private updateComet(socket) {
    // double-check to see if we do have a comet. Bit of
    defensive programming
    if (this.hasComet) {
        // Generate random numbers, but always make sure
        these are
        // offscreen, or the user will see a comet for a
        split-second
        // on-screen and then disappear to the correct spot.
        let asteroidCoordinates = this.
        generateRandomCoordinates();
```

```
    // Move the comet offscreen based on the sprite's
    initial height
    asteroidCoordinates.y = -128;

    const update = setInterval(() => {
        // after 25 milliseconds we update the comet's
        x- and y-values
        // to illustrate an animation in time. This
        allows for
        // smooth scrolling from the top to the bottom
        of the screen.
        asteroidCoordinates.y += 1;
        asteroidCoordinates.x -= 1;

        // broadcast to the clients about the right
        coordinates
        socket.emit(CometEvent.coordinates,
        asteroidCoordinates);
        socket.broadcast.emit(
            CometEvent.coordinates,
            asteroidCoordinates
        );

        // in this loop we shall be checking if we need
        to ever
        // destroy the comet as well. This makes it
        more efficient
        // for us as the life cycle is all in one place.
        this.destroyComet(asteroidCoordinates, socket,
        update)
    }, 25);
  }
}
```

```
private destroyComet(asteroidCoordinates, socket, update):
void {
    // if we detect that the comet is out of bounds. We
    then move in to
    // change the comet boolean to false. This will be
    caught by our
    // interval trigger to create a new one, and we reset
    the boolean
    // value to true.
    if (asteroidCoordinates.x < -128) {
        this.hasComet = false;

        // update the clients with the destroy method for
        them to remove
        // their sprites accordingly.
        socket.emit(CometEvent.destroy);
        socket.broadcast.emit(CometEvent.destroy);

        // clear the update interval to free up memory and
        also to not
        // have two or more different streams of asteroids
        being
        // generated, we only want one of these. Not
        removing the
        // interval will result in the server mismatching
        with the
        // client and the client flickering between the
        newly created
```

```
        // instances of comets. A buggy experience indeed
        global.clearInterval(update);
    }
  }

  // ...
}
```

Nice! If all went according to plan, you now have killer asteroids/comets or giant rocks of doom waiting to crush your little ship as soon as you touch them! We can better distinguish our player from the enemy players as well in our game.

Let's add a special sprite for the protagonist, which is the blue ship we have. But since every player from their perspective will be a protagonist, it's good to have control of who will get the blue or the red ship! Grab the player.class.ts file and let's make the following modifications (see Listing 9-7).

Listing 9-7. src/client/actors/player/player.class.ts

```
import {KeyBoardControl} from '../../controls/keyboard.class';
import {Projectile} from '../../props/powers/projectile/
projectile.class';
import {Hud} from '../../hud/hud.class';
import {Particle} from '../../props/particle/particle.class';
import {SpaceShip} from '../../../shared/models';
import {Explode} from '../../props/explosion/explosion.class';

export class Player {
    public player: Phaser.Sprite;
    public projectile: Projectile;
    public controls: KeyBoardControl;
    public playerState: Map<string, boolean | number>;
```

```
public hud: Hud;
public angularVelocity: number = 300;
private particle: Particle;

// add the type argument here as well!
constructor(private gameInstance: Phaser.Game,
            public playerInstance: SpaceShip, type) {

    // pass the type as a value
    this.createPlayer(this.gameInstance, type);
    this.playerState = new Map();
}

// We shall pass the type argument to the creation of the
player through
// this method
public createPlayer(gameInstance, type): void {
    this.hud = new Hud();
    this.addControls();

    // modify the sprite form we shall be taking with a
    type argument
    this.player = gameInstance.add.sprite(this.
    playerInstance.x,
        this.playerInstance.y, type);
    this.player.id = this.playerInstance.id;
    this.player.anchor.setTo(0.5, 0.5);
    this.player.animations.add('accelerating', [1, 0], 60,
    false);
    this.player.name = this.playerInstance.name;
    this.attachPhysics(gameInstance);
```

```
    this.player.destroy = () => {
        new Explode(this.gameInstance, this.player);
        this.player.kill();
    }

    this.hud.setName(gameInstance, this.player);
    this.particle = new Particle(gameInstance, this.player);
}

public assignPickup(game, player?): void {
    this.projectile = new Projectile(game, player.player);
    this.hud.setAmmo(game, player.player, this.projectile);
    this.playerState.set('ammo', this.projectile.bulletCount);
}

public view(): void {
    this.controls.update();
    if (this.projectile) {
        this.hud.update(this.playerState.get('ammo'));
    }
}

private addControls(): void {
    this.controls = new KeyBoardControl(this.gameInstance,
    this);
}

private attachPhysics(gameInstance): void {
    gameInstance.physics.enable(this.player, Phaser.
    Physics.ARCADE);
    this.player.body.collideWorldBounds = true;
    this.player.body.bounce.setTo(10, 10);
    this.player.body.gravity.y = 0;
    this.player.body.drag.set(80);
```

```
        this.player.body.maxVelocity.set(100);
        this.player.body.immovable = false;
    }

}
```

We are one step closer to having real enemies! It's not ethical to shoot at our own colored banners!

Listing 9-8. src/client/game/game.class.ts

```
// ...
export class Game {

    protected manageAssets(game): void {
        // modify your player create scripts to have a ship
        type.
        window.socket.on(PlayerEvent.joined, (player) => {
            this.actors.push(new Player(game, player, 'shooter-
            sprite-enemy'));
        });

        // and here!
        window.socket.on(PlayerEvent.protagonist, (player) => {
            this.actor = new Player(game, player, 'shooter-
            sprite');
            this.actors.push(this.actor);
        });

        // here three!
        window.socket.on(PlayerEvent.players, (players) => {
            players.map((player: any) => {
                const enemy = new Player(game, player,
                'shooter-sprite-enemy');
```

```
        if (player.ammo) {
            enemy.assignPickup(game, enemy);
        }
        this.actors.push(enemy);
    });
});

// ...
}

}
```

Last, but definitely not least, we are going to touch the engine class in order to add the evil sprite! This way we can distinguish between evil enemy ships and ourselves. This would also work for the other player. You will then appear red on her screen and blue on your own.

Listing 9-9. src/client/engine/phaser-engine.class.ts

```
import { Game } from "../game/game.class";
import { LifeCycle } from "./lifecycle";

export class PhaserSpaceGame extends Game implements Life Cycle {

    private game: Phaser.Game;

    constructor() {
        super();
        this.game = new Phaser.Game(1024, 768, Phaser.AUTO,
        'space-shooter', {
            preload: this.preload,
            create: this.create,
            update: this.update
        });
    }
```

```
public preload(): void {
    const game = this.game.load;
    game.crossOrigin = 'anonymous';
    game.image('space', 'assets/background.jpg');
    game.image('laser', 'assets/bullet.png');
    game.spritesheet('dust', 'assets/dust.png', 64, 64, 16);
    game.spritesheet('kaboom', 'assets/explosions.png', 64,
    64, 16);
    game.image('pickup', 'assets/pickup.png');
    game.spritesheet('shooter-sprite', 'assets/ship.png',
    32, 32);

    // add the new evil sprite!
    // Feel free to use any graphic you have and place it
    inside of the
    // assets folder with the name mentioned below. If you
    cannot
    // think of anything, you can use the provided sprite
    in the main
    // branch of this github repository.
    game.spritesheet(
        'shooter-sprite-enemy',
        'assets/ship-enemy.png', 32, 32
    );
}

public create(): void {
    super.properties(this.game);
    super.manageAssets(this.game);
}
```

```
public update(): void {
    super.gameUpdate(this.game);
}

}
```

Conclusion

That concludes our adventure in space for this time. In the next chapter, we finish off the ride with some souvenirs from the world and places you can keep leveling up your skills. Changes and updates will happen just on the free github repo. Check for the latest features added to the game by starring the repo so you will automatically track and watch for changes. The latest addition added was the ability to destroy the asteroid once it has been fired!

The book's final code and repo are found on the following link: https://github.com/codeOwl/Multiplayer-Phaser-game.

CHAPTER 10

Further Reading And Discovery

Congratulations and I hope you have learned a lot by following me through this short book. Use this as a guide or a template if you are interested in creating more multiplayer games out there. Following me on Twitter and github will give me more energy to help others with the knowledge I have gained in my career. Thank you for your support, and I really appreciate you for taking the time to read and hopefully learn from this material.

My upcoming book will be covering the same material but using the newly created Phaser 3 framework. I will be making a completely different game, but it will also be a multiplayer game.

Other Phaser Resources

Here is a comprehensive list of materials that have helped me and others keep up-to-date with Phaser. Having these in your arsenal will make you build much better, more technically sound games if you are using the Phaser framework!

If you are stuck or need help with anything, please just create an issue on the github page of the game and I or the community around this book will help resolve that (`https://github.com/codeOwl/Multiplayer-Phaser-game/issues`).

© Oscar Lodriguez 2019
O. Lodriguez, *Let's Build a Multiplayer Phaser Game*,
https://doi.org/10.1007/978-1-4842-4249-0_10

The online repo of this game:

- `https://github.com/codeOwl/Multiplayer- .`
  `Phaser-game`

Awesome github repo:

- `https://github.com/Raiper34/awesome-phaser`

Phaser's personal shop:

- `https://phaser.io/shop`

Phaser tutorials:

- `https://phaser.io/learn/official-tutorials`

Phaser examples:

- `https://phaser.io/examples`

Interphase:

- `https://phaser.io/interphase`

Index

A, B

Arcade model, 36, 38–39
Asteroid
    class creation, 130–131
    comet specific events, 133–139
    engine class, 143–145
    game class, 131–133, 142–143
    player class, 139–141

C

Client side, game, 98–106
Comet specific events, 133

D

Development setup
    code editors, 7
    dev mode, 9
    folder structure, 10–11
    front-end architecture, 9–10
    installing Git, 6
    installing Node.js, 5–6
    project, dev mode, 9
    project, run, 8–9
Directory
    construction, 23
    creation, 21–22

Domain model
    game class, 15–16
    keyboard class, 17, 19
    player class, 16–17

E

Explosion
    class creation, 107–108
    projectile class, 108–109

F

Front-end architecture, 9–10

G

Game engine file
    import index, 56
    imports, code, 50–51
    keyboard class
        code, 54–56
    player class
        code, 51–52, 54
Game model, 40–41, 43
Git, 6, 7
    clone command, 22
Github, 2, 7

© Oscar Lodriguez 2019
O. Lodriguez, *Let's Build a Multiplayer Phaser Game*,
https://doi.org/10.1007/978-1-4842-4249-0

Printed in the United States
By Bookmasters